Chinese Vegetarian Cooking
WOK WISELY

by the Dharma Realm Cookbook Team of Taiwan

Buddhist Text Translation Society
2015

WOK WISELY

Chinese Vegetarian Cooking
A monastery's approach to food and spiritual well-being—
adding eastern variety and peace of mind and body.

Adapted from Caigen piaoxiang—fajie shipu 1 菜根飄香-法界食譜 1, 2006.

Editorial Team: Bhikshuni Jin Rou, Ella Fitzbag, Joann Henderson, Cynthia Mossman, Greg Lau, Toni Minor, Desi Bisel

Design by Bhikshuni Jin Gwo

Published and translated by:
Buddhist Text Translation Society

©2015 Buddhist Text Translation Society,
Dharma Realm Buddhist University,
Dharma Realm Buddhist Association

Buddhist Text Translation Society
4951 Bodhi Way, Ukiah, CA 95482
www.buddhisttexts.org
info@buddhisttexts.org

Printed on acid-free paper in Taiwan

Note: Pinyin is used for the romanization of Chinese words, except in proper names which retain familiar romanizations.

The publisher has generously been given permission to use charts and extended quotations from Healing with Whole Foods: Asian Traditions and Modern Tradition, Third Edition, by Paul Pitchford, published by North Atlantic Books, copyright ©2002 by Paul Pitchford. Reprinted by permission of the publisher.

Library of Congress Cataloging-in-Publication Data
Fa jie shi pu gong zuo qun (Taiwan)
  [880-01 Cai gen piao xiang. English.]
  Wok wisely : Chinese vegetarian cooking : a monastery's approach to food and spiritual well-being : adding Eastern variety and peace of mind and body / by the Dharma Realm Cookbook Team of Taiwan.
     pages cm
  Translation of: Cai gen piao xiang.
  Includes bibliographical references.
  ISBN 978-1-60103-075-7 (alk. paper)
  1. Vegetarian cooking. 2. Food—Religious aspects—Buddhism. 3. Cooking, Chinese. I. Dharma Realm Buddhist Association. II. Buddhist Text Translation Society. III. Title.
  TX837.F23513 2015
  641.5951—dc23

助印單位：財團法人法界文教基金會
Printing Sponsored by:Dharma Realm Buddhist Cultural Education Foundation

2014033153

CONTENTS

FOREWORD

The Buddha taught that all creatures with consciousness, blood and breath are kin. We are all members of a family connected in substance and nature. Buddhists have always maintained that animals have feelings and that killing them causes unnecessary grief and suffering. Nobody suffers willingly; harm done to one hurts all alike. Chinese Buddhists incorporate the principle of kindness into the practice of meatless, cruelty-free eating. All creatures are our family, and we don't eat our kin.

The spiritual well-being of humanity on earth is tied to the well-being of animals just as they are. Animals have a place at the table, not on the table. Seen this way, cows are not steak or burgers or veal; pigs are not bacon or chops or ribs. Fish are not fillets or chowder or seafood. Even the smallest of creatures deserves and receives respect. Size is not the standard that determines their right to live; their right to live is a fundamental condition.

—Reverend Heng Sure, Ph.D,
 Berkeley Buddhist Monastery
 Chairperson, Buddhist Text
 Translation Society

PEACE BEGINS WITH A VEGETARIAN DIET

by Venerable Master Hsuan Hua (1918–1995)

Taking life includes taking one's own life, telling others to take life, or taking delight in witnessing the taking of life. One of the reasons that wars rage in the world is because we take each other's lives. An ancient Chinese poem says:

> *For countless years the bitter stew of hate goes boiling on.*
> *Its vengeful broth is ocean deep, impossible to calm.*
> *To learn the cause of all this conflict,*
> *Terror, bombs and war,*
> *Listen to the cries at midnight by the butcher's door.*

—Chan Master Cloud of Vows (Song Dynasty, 960–1279) from *Kindness*

The grief and hatred brewed up in a pot of meat stew is as deep as the ocean. It could never be fully described. The wars and massacres in the world are brought about by the accumulation of the evil karma of living beings, causing them to undergo vengeance at the same time. If you listen carefully to the cries of misery coming from a slaughterhouse in the middle of the night, you will realize the horror of the ceaseless killing that occurs there.

Scientists have discovered that people who eat a great deal of meat tend to get cancer. This is because the resentful energy in the bodies of slaughtered animals accumulates in the bodies of those who eat meat and eventually turns into a harmful toxin. We should cut off this relationship of cause and effect with animals and stop the vicious

cycle of creating offenses against cows, sheep, chickens, and other animals. Then we will gradually be able to lessen the inauspicious energy in the world.

At the City of Ten Thousand Buddhas, we want to avert the crisis of killing in the world. We want to slowly and imperceptibly avert this disaster. Therefore we advocate: not killing, not stealing, not engaging in sexual misconduct, not lying, not drinking alcohol, and not taking illicit drugs. Since you have come to this treasure mountain, don't leave empty handed!

From a talk given on November 20, 1979 at the City of 10,000 Buddhas, Talmage, California

NOTE FROM THE AUTHORS

The *History of the Former Han* [a classical history completed in III CE, covering the history of China under the Western Han dynasty from 206 BCE to 25 CE] states: "Food is the basis of life." Food has generally been a topic of interest to people. Confucius once said, "Do not eat food that looks bad. Do not eat food that smells bad. Do not eat at the wrong time." Do we think about why we eat, how we select our food?

In Buddhism food is called "medicine." In the early stages of Chinese medicine, food was the most important cure. Chinese herbal medicine was originally referred to as soup. One of the earliest writings on Chinese medicine, *Plain Questions*, rarely made reference to herbal medicine, but adjustments to diets were mentioned frequently.

Eating does not merely extend our life — it helps us develop stronger and healthier bodies, so that we can realize our ideals and contribute to our society. Human ideals are grounded in a respect for life. However, with modern technology that allows food to be mass produced and distributed globally, it has lost its seasonal or local qualities.

On the other hand, there is a rising interest in organic methods that combine scientific knowledge and modern technology with traditional farming practices based on thousands of years of agriculture. In general, organic farming is a practice of cultivation of crops that involves eco-friendly methods that avoid the use of inorganic products such as chemical fertilizers, insecticides, herbicides, fungicides and pesticides. At present organic farming is being practiced across the world on a large scale, covering millions of hectares of land.

Healthy eating is holistic, taking care of both the body and spirit. Food pleases the physical senses and extends life. Chinese ancients classified the flavors of food into five categories: sour, sweet, bitter, spicy, and salty. They believed that different flavors can strengthen different organs. The Chinese often say, "What you eat is what you become." The well-known phrase in English is, "You are what you eat."

In Buddhism, the saying, "Great kindness requires no special circumstances and great compassion comes from seeing one as all." This saying refers to the absence of discrimination and the ability to empathize with other beings. Thinking about food like this, our life will become increasingly calm and peaceful, and we will grow in wisdom.

All his life the Venerable Master Hsuan Hua lived by these six guiding principles: not fighting, not being greedy, not seeking outside, not being selfish, not pursuing personal advantage, and not lying. In the spirit of upholding these principles, a well-known chef, Guo Guan, and our cooking team decided to make an offering to Buddhism by publishing a series of vegetarian cookbooks — to spare the lives of animals and to protect them instead. With a few desk lamps, pieces of fabric, and a digital camera, we created a studio in the corner of the dining hall of the Dharma Realm Monastery in Taiwan. Volunteer cooks brought their best dishes for everyone to taste during the Dharma gatherings. We decorated the dishes with tiny flowers and curly vegetable leaves, transforming them into beautiful delicacies that we offered in a Buddhist ceremony to the Buddha.

Guo Guan is a renowned chef in the Taiwanese culinary world. He has received praise from two former presidents and other government officials in Taiwan, who testify to his superb cooking. After meeting the Venerable Master Hsuan Hua, Guo Guan became a Buddhist and a vegetarian. Since then, he has dedicated himself to promoting a plant-based diet throughout the world.

The purpose of these cookbooks is to foster a fresh outlook on respecting life and to inspire everyone to make better choices in their diet and lifestyle. This first volume, *Wok Wisely*, presents the best of healthy traditional Chinese cooking. It includes fifty-six recipes that are easy enough for the beginner, yet rich enough in variety for the professional. The second volume, *The World of Cooking*, with more than sixty recipes, requires more culinary experience. The other volumes are collections of recipes that, before publication, were known only to Guo Guan himself. All these dishes are meant to engender a feeling for the freedom of creating new taste delights that reinforce the good health found in vegetarian cooking.

These recipes are meant to show how versatile, colorful, and flavorful Chinese vegetarian food can be. Explanations are given about the ingredients so that those unfamiliar with Chinese food will know what they are eating and what to look for in the Asian sections of grocery stores. In addition, useful information about protecting and supporting health is provided along with quotes from famous vegetarians. All of this is intended to inspire readers to make the earth a better place for all who live upon it.

NOTE: The Buddha recommended that animals and animal products, pungent plants, and intoxicants be avoided by Buddhist practitioners, because of their adverse effects on consciousness. For this reason, none of the recipes contain any of the five pungent pltants: leeks, onions, chives, garlic, and shallots.

The beauty of vegetarianism
Lies in its simplicity and delight.
It is about enjoying good taste,
It is about being happy and serene.

Kept warm by cotton cloth,
Nourished by vegetable roots—
One savors the constant study of the classics.
Kind and compassionate in thought,
Joyful and good at heart—
One delights in the virtue of being vegetarian.

—Dharma Realm Cookbook Team

COOKING
FOR HEALTH
AND A CLEAR
CONSCIENCE

Showing gratitude toward all living beings is the foundation of life.

A. Dietary Information for Vegetarians

I. PROTEIN

Protein is important for building bones, muscles, and blood cells, and for providing digestive enzymes and antioxidant enzymes. It is made up of amino acids, some that our bodies can make by utilizing the nutrition that we consume, but there are eight other essential amino acids that our bodies cannot synthesize and must obtain from other food sources. A variety of grains, legumes (beans, peas, lentils) and soy products, such as tempeh and tofu, vegetables, and seaweed, can provide all of these essential acids and safely double the amount that animal protein would provide.

Most people think that plants do not contain protein, and even some vegetarians think that beans are the only vegetable with protein. Calories in food come from protein, fat, and carbohydrates. The chart below shows the percentage of protein in food calories for some common foods.

Plant-Based Food Rich in Protein

Protein in grams per 100 grams (3½ ounce) edible portion Protein (g)

All fruits	.2 – 2		Nuts and Seeds	
Vegetables			Filberts	13
Carrots	1		Almonds	19
Cabbage	1		Sesame seeds	19
Cauliflower	3		Sunflower seeds	24
Broccoli	4		**Legumes**	
Kale	4		Aduki beans	22
Parsley	4		Dry peas	24
Brussels sprouts	5		Lentils	25
Grains			Soybeans	35
Rice	7		**Seaweed**	
Barley	8		Agar-agar	2
Corn	9		Hijiki	6
Rye	9		Kombu	7
Millet	10		Wakame	13
Buckwheat	12		Kelp	16
Oats	13		Dulse	22
Amaranth	16		Nori	35
Quinoa	18		Nutritional Yeast	50

SOURCE: Paul Pitchford, *Healing with Whole Foods*, (Berkeley: North Atlantic Books, 2002). Used by permission.

Over the last thirty years, research studies have concurred that over-consumption of protein greatly puts one at risk for kidney failure and bone loss (osteoporosis). The correlation between cancer and excess protein is also recognized by many medical professionals. Over-consumption of any form of protein, not just animal protein and concentrated plant protein, can be a risk. The ideal consumption of concentrated protein should be between 2.5 and 8.0 percent of one's total diet.

2. CALCIUM

Most vegetables and legumes contain more than adequate amounts of calcium. See the chart below:

Plant-Based Food Rich in Calcium

Food	Calcium in Milligrams
Hijiki	1400
Wakame	1300
Kelp	1099
Kombu	800
Agar-Agar	400
Nori	260
Almonds	333
Amaranth grain	222
Hazelnuts	209
Parsley	203
Turnip greens	191
Brazil nuts	186
Sunflower seeds	174
Watercress	151
Garbanzo beans	150
Quinoa	141
Black beans	135
Pistachios	135
Pinto beans	135
Kale	134
Collard greens	117
Sesame seeds	110
Chinese cabbage	106
Tofu	100
Walnuts	99
Okra	82
Brown rice	33

SOURCE: Paul Pitchford, *Healing with Whole Foods*, (Berkeley: North Atlantic Books, 2002). Used by permission.

Barley, oats, potatoes, wheat, asparagus, artichokes, broccoli, butternut squash, sweet potatoes, dried figs, oranges, raspberries, apples, and pears are also rich in calcium.

Getting enough calcium is usually not a problem. The difficulty is in effectively absorbing and utilizing it. All the minerals in the body are in a delicate balance. If a deficiency in calcium exists, other minerals will also be out of balance. Below are some recommendations for increasing calcium absorption and to improve the health effects of minerals:

1. **Get sufficient vitamin D from sunshine.** The ideal amount of exposure is at least twenty percent of the skin for fifteen minutes a day at sea level, but not at midday. The sun needs to shine on the face, hands, and lower arms, because this is where the sun receptors are located. Cloudy days and glass windows cut down on the amount of vitamin D the skin makes.

2. **Eat calcium, magnesium, chlorophyll, and mineral-rich foods**—grains, legumes, leafy greens such as kale and collards, seaweed, cereal grasses, and/or micro-algae.

3. **Avoid calcium inhibitors such as:**
   Coffee, soft drinks, and diuretics
   Alcohol, marijuana, tobacco, and other intoxicants
   Excess protein and salt
   Refined sugar and excess concentrated sweeteners

4. **Limit use of foods that bind calcium such as:**
   Solanine foods: potatoes, eggplants, bell peppers, tomatoes
   Oxalic foods: rhubarb, cranberries, plums, chard, beet greens

5. **Presoak grains and legumes before cooking.** This will neutralize their phytic content, which otherwise binds the minerals in these foods. Discard soaking water.

6. **Exercise regularly and moderately.** Stand and walk often. Bones need to bear weight and exert force against gravity to prevent loss of calcium.

3. VITAMIN B12 IN THE VEGAN DIET

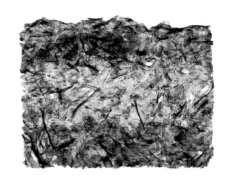

Vitamin B12 is an essential part of the human diet. The only known source of this vitamin comes from bacterial micro-organisms found in soil and water. We do not produce vitamin B12 in our bodies as we do other vitamins, and we do not get it from plants, unless they are contaminated with bacteria from soil and water or supplemented with vitamin B12. Animals are a source of vitamin B12, because these bacteria are found in their plant foods. For this reason, vegans need to look to fortified foods or supplements to get vitamin B12 in their diet.

Why do we need B12?

To form and maintain healthy blood and nerve cells and to make DNA, the genetic material in cells.

What happens if we don't get enough B12?

1. Fatigue, breathlessness, listlessness, and poor resistance to infection
2. Numbness and tingling in the hands and feet
3. Depression, confusion, dementia, poor memory
4. Delayed growth in infants, also movement disorders, and anemia
5. Other problems such as constipation, loss of appetite, weight loss, and difficulty keeping one's balance.

How much B12 do we need daily?

It depends on your age. The dosage will be on the container, but in general, the average daily recommended amounts for adults is 2.4 mcg and 2.6 mcg for pregnant teens and women. Ask your physician to recommend amounts for children. Consuming high amounts of B12 has not been shown to be harmful.

What are good vegetarian sources of B12?

Adults should include at least three good sources of vitamin B12 in their diets each day. It is best to include a variety of different fortified foods in your diet, rather than relying solely on one source. Examples of good sources of B12 include:

- Fortified foods such as cereal, nut and grain milk; these are made with the B12–producing bacteria, and not animal products.
- Nutritional yeast such as Red Yeast vegetarian support formula
- Vitamin B12 dietary supplements

Do pickles and fermented foods like miso, tempeh, and soy sauce contain B12?

According to research, vitamin B12-producing bacteria are not required for fermented food. If fermented food contains vitamin B12, it is due to high levels of contamination.

What about seaweed, mushrooms, and root vegetables?

Since vitamin B12 is produced by micro-organisms in soil, mushrooms and root vegetables contain adequate amounts of B12. If all the dirt is not washed off, they are a good source of B12. Most people clean their vegetables so well that all traces are removed. Seaweed contains B12 analogues, which are not vitamin B12. Unpasteurized sauerkraut and sprouts aid in the ingestion of B12 by replenishing and conditioning the good bacteria.

4. ALKALINE BALANCE

The body should be slightly alkaline in order to build an alkaline reserve for acid-forming conditions such as stress, poor diet, or lack of exercise. An acid-alkaline balance is important for normal cell function. The most alkaline-producing foods are fruits, vegetables, sprouts, whole grains, and herbs, which also help preserve the bones. A beneficial acid and alkaline balance can also be achieved by other methods such as:

- Soaking whole grains and legumes for six to seven hours before cooking them to start the sprouting process, which is alkalizing. Discard the soaking water and add fresh water before cooking.

- Thoroughly chewing complex carbohydrates such as grains, vegetables, and legumes in order to mix them with saliva to begin the digestive process. Saliva is very alkaline.

- Do not drink liquids while eating. This stops the digestive process from beginning within the mouth.

- Adapting a moderate lifestyle with exercise, spiritual practice, and a high level of positive thinking. Exercise tends to make the body more alkaline, but excessive exercise will become acid-forming.

5. NUTRITION FOR VEGETARIAN CHILDREN

"Diet, Children and the Future" by Dr. John McDougall, McDougall Newsletter, September 2012

In the article above, Dr. McDougall says,

"One need not worry about children getting enough protein, calcium, iron, zinc, essential amino acids and fats as long as they are eating a starch-based diet of potatoes, corn, rice, beans, etc. Mother's milk is 5.5 percent protein and naturally provides children with the right amount of nourishment when they are growing the fastest. Once children are weaned, they get their nutrition in the same way as adults, however, children must be provided with sufficient calories for growth by adding a variety of vegetables and concentrated foods such as dried fruits, nuts, seeds, nut butters, and avocados. Fruit and vegetable juices are also loaded with calories. Parents and children should become familiar with nutritional facts in order to maintain good health."

Dr. McDougall is the author of the McDougall Program that outlines how diet can reverse common diseases. Reference to the entire article: https://www.drmcdougall.com/misc/2012nl/sep/children.htm

B. Where to Buy Ingredients for Chinese Cooking

One of the first things you'll want to know when preparing to make a Chinese recipe is where to find the ingredients. With the growing interest in ethnic foods, many items are now widely available in the Asian sections of supermarkets or in health food stores. Below is a handy list of the most commonly used Chinese ingredients. Information about these ingredients can be found with the recipes that use them. Special items may call for a trip to a Chinese/Asian market or online ordering.

Anise Stars

Bamboo Shoots

Bok Choy

Chinese Cabbage

Daikon Radish

Edamame

Five-Spice Powder

Gingerroot

Gluten Balls, fried

Gluten Balls, ground chunks

Gluten Rolls, (Gluten Puff)

Goji Berries

Green Peas

Kelp and Kombu Seaweed

Miso

Mung Beans

Noodles (many different types are available)

Nori Seaweed

Rice Vinegar

Shitake Mushrooms, fresh and dried

Soybean Sprouts

Soy Sauce, dark or light

Tofu

Wasabi Japanese Mustard

Water Chestnuts

C. Wholesome Ingredients That Support Health

I. NATURAL THICKENERS
Used for sauces, soups, fruit pie fillings and glazes, and puddings.

Agar powder	A seaweed extract used like gelatin; has a firm texture and does not melt easily; low in calories; promotes digestion and weight loss
Arrowroot powder	A white powder extracted from the root of a West Indian plant; transparent; no flavor; draws out toxins
Kudzu powder	Smooth and transparent; less likely to harden; cools and soothes the stomach and intestines
Yam flour	Somewhat transparent and elastic; congeals and hardens
Lotus root flour	Smooth, transparent and elastic; contains calcium

2. NATURAL SWEETENERS

According to Chinese medicine one should avoid an excess of any flavor, especially the sweet flavor. Overconsumption of refined sugars crowds out more nutritious foods and disperses the life force. Calcium is lost from the system, causing bone problems. The digestive system is weakened and food cannot be assimilated properly. This leads to a blood-sugar imbalance and a further craving for sugar.

In the context of a healthy, whole food based diet, small amounts of natural sugar-based sweeteners won't cause harm, especially in baked goods with healthy ingredients. These sweeteners can be used like white sugar in baking, stove-top cooking, and in beverages, and may be considered useful for people with diabetes. Those containing maltose are less destructive to the body's mineral balance and are recommended for infant formulas.

Unrefined Sweeteners	Source	Quantity
Substitute Ratio to 1 cup sugar		
Amasake	Fermented rice; 40% maltose	1½ cups
Barbados/Sorghum Molasses	Cooked-down cane juice; 65% sucrose	⅓ cup
Barley Malt/ Rice Syrup/ Maltose	Sprouted grains; 50% maltose	1⅓ cups
Maple Syrup	Boiled down maple tree sap; high in calcium; 65% sucrose	⅔ cup
Rapadura	Unrefined cane juice powder; 82% sucrose; contains a few nutrients	½–1 cups
Refined Sweeteners	**Source**	**Quantity**
Agave Syrup	Agave plant; 90% fructose, low glycemic level	¼ cup
Brown Sugar	White sugar with molasses; 100% sucrose	1 cup
Raw Sugar/Rock Sugar	Dehydrated cane juice; slightly less refined; 99% sucrose	1 cup
White Sugar	corn, sugar cane, or sugar beets; 100% sucrose	

3. COOKING OILS

Oils add flavor to food, so it's good to have a variety on hand. Regardless of the oil, it should be unrefined and at best, organic and cold-pressed or expeller-pressed. The oil will then retain its original taste, nutrients and vitamin E content, which prevents the oil from becoming rancid. The color will sometimes be cloudy.

There are three categories of oils: monounsaturated, saturated and polyunsaturated. All oils contain all three categories but are classified by the type of fatty acid that makes up most of the oil.

Monounsaturated oils lower cholesterol and have a more positive effect on health than other oils do. Olive and peanut oils, as well as most nut and avocado oils, are monounsaturated. Extra-virgin olive oil is expeller-pressed and high in antioxidants that are linked to heart health, but "pure" olive oil is refined and does not contain antioxidants. Since monounsaturated oils have a high fat content, it is good advice to cut down on the amount of these oils in the diet to ensure overall health.

Saturated oils are considered the most stable and do not easily turn rancid. Saturated oils include coconut, palm kernel, and cocoa butter. For added benefit, eat the whole coconut along with the oil, either shredded or as milk or flour.

Polyunsaturated oils are the most problematic ones. They include the typical flavorless oils with long shelf lives that have been refined beyond their ability to offer nutrients and energy to our bodies. The high temperatures transform the fatty acids into a synthetic fat called "trans-fatty acids." Recent research shows that these trans-fatty acids raise the level of blood cholesterol, increasing the risk of arthritis, cancer, and heart disease. Polyunsaturated oils include corn, canola, sesame, soybean, sunflower and cottonseed oils. Some of these oils like sesame, soybean and sunflower can be found organically grown and expeller-pressed.

Caution

Some people are allergic to nut and soy oil. An even more serious situation arises when these oils are re-used for deep frying, typically in restaurants.

Tips for using oil

- Flax, hemp, walnut, and sunflower oils should not be heated as they produce toxins: Use them in salads or drizzle over cooked food.
- Olive, sesame and almond oils are less toxic when baked or sautéed at low temperatures.
- Coconut, palm, peanut, and soybean oils can be widely used for frying as they produce the least toxic substances.

4. SALT

The use of salt is as old as human history. Dr. Jacques de Langre, in *Sea Salt's Hidden Powers*, discusses more than forty kinds of salt and how they are harvested. The most common salts used in cooking today are sea salt and table salt. Sea salt is harvested from seawater through evaporation. Table salt is ground rock salt that is mined from mineral deposits, but both types of salt can be fully refined. Table salt often contains added iodine, necessary for normal thyroid function. Sea salt naturally contains iodine, but in lesser amounts than table salt, but there are plenty of sources of iodine available in vegetarian food. Whole sea salt is slightly grey and is a source of twenty-one essential and thirty additional minerals that are important to our health. Refined salt is almost pure sodium chloride. It also contains additives, such as anti-caking chemicals and sugar, and has a negative effect on our health. Beware of the label "sea salt" on packaged food in supermarkets and health food stores. Originally, it may have come from the sea, but it may have been refined. Look for the word "unrefined" on the label.

In Chinese medicine, salt detoxifies the body and regulates its water content, strengthens the digestion, and helps move the bowels. Salt has a "grounding" effect on the body and strengthens one's energy.

Salt should enhance and not dominate the flavor of food. If the food has a salty taste, it is too much. Salt should be cooked into food and not added at the table, so it will be better distributed through the food. Reactions to salt vary greatly from person to person. Overall, most people use too much, especially when adding their own. Even a little sprinkle would be overdoing it.

Overuse of any kind of salt, including soy sauce and miso, can cause calcium depletion and damage the heart, arteries, nerves, bones, kidneys, and muscles. Excess salt, in Chinese folklore, is thought to encourage greed and hostility.

READILY AVAILABLE SAFE HOUSEHOLD CLEANSERS

- Commercial cleaners contain toxic substances like formaldehyde, phosphates, ammonia, chlorine bleach, arsenic, and sulfuric acid, just to name a few. When breathed in, these chemicals enter into the entire respiratory system and leach into the blood stream, leaving traces in the heart and other organs (cancer causing). They also release volatile organic compounds (VOCs) that pollute the air inside our homes.

- Unfortunately, they end up going down the drain and into streams, rivers, and other water sources, where they kill aquatic life. Seeping into the ground, they contaminate vegetation and rise to pollute the air.

- Most cleansers are tested on animals. When purchasing them, always check the labels for no testing on animals. The good news is that the safest household cleansers can be found on kitchen shelves around the world. Below are some recipes for making your own cleansers for a healthy and clean environment:

  All-Purpose Cleanser: Mix a solution of equal parts of vinegar and water in a spray bottle.

  Scrub: Mix lemon juice with baking soda and make a paste.

  Furniture Polish: Mix one cup olive oil with ½ cup lemon juice

  To unclog drains: Pour three cups boiling water, one cup baking soda and one cup vinegar down the drain.

  Bleach: Use hydrogen peroxide instead of chlorine bleach.

EWG's *Guide to Healthy Cleaning* www.ewg.org/guides/cleaners, Sep 10, 2012

Griffin, R. Morgan, (reviewed by Michael W. Smith, MD). *Keeping Your House Clean Without Harsh Chemicals.* www.webmd.com/children/exposure/safer-cleaning-product

D. Cooking Methods and Cookware

Not overcooking vegetables retains at least ninety percent of their vitamins and nutrients. Always cook with filtered water.

Methods

- **Blanching:** Quickly boil vegetables until bright green. Immediately rinse with cold water and drain. This helps to retain the color and to remove bitterness.

- **Braising:** Cook vegetables over high heat, gently stirring. Add small amounts of water at a time until vegetables are covered.

- **Frying:** Heat oil in a deep fryer to 350 degrees or until a cube of bread browns within thirty seconds. Fry ingredients, in batches, for one to two minutes, until golden. Drain on absorbent towels.

- **Oven-frying:** Brush vegetables with oil, and then bake.

- **Stir-frying:** Heat a wok until hot. Add oil and swirl the pan around to cover entire surface. Do not let oil smoke. Add ginger or other spices to flavor the oil. Then add main ingredients, but not all at once so temperature does not drop. Toss, flip, and swish with long chopsticks or a wooden spoon to coat with oil so the natural flavors are sealed in, and to prevent scorching. This gives stir-fried dishes great spirit.

- **Final seasoning:** At the end of cooking, add a thickener dissolved in water, or a few drops of sesame oil for an aromatic sheen. Give ingredients a few fast turns over high heat to glaze them well.

> **TIP:** A stir-fried dish is never watery except for those meant to be saucy. Remove from wok immediately so the food doesn't turn dark or have a metallic taste. Serve in a heated dish.

- **Sautéing:** A tasty, quick method using a little oil to seal in the natural flavors and juices. Heat a heavy skillet and brush with oil. Keep a medium-high heat and add vegetables. Gently toss side to side with chopsticks or a wooden spoon for about five minutes. For softer vegetables, cover and cook over medium heat for about ten minutes.

- **Water Stir-fry (without oil):** Rub the bottom of a heavy skillet or wok with a three-inch piece of soaked kombu seaweed. Leave in the pan to prevent sticking. (Remove at end of cooking.) Heat the skillet and stir-fry or sauté vegetables by the usual method. Add a little water if you like.

- **Water and Oil Stir-fry:** Has the flavor of stir-fry without overheating the oil. Cover the bottom of a heavy skillet or wok with water and then heat. Drizzle with oil and stir-fry or sauté vegetables by the usual method.

- **Pan-roasting:** Heat pan and add ingredients. Swish the pan around or stir with a wooden spoon to prevent scorching.

- **Simmering:** Bring food to a boil, cover and reduce heat to low. Cook slowly until food is tender.

- **Steaming:** Steaming adds a moist quality and brings out the flavor of vegetables; short cooking time. Arrange the ingredients in a steamer and place in a pot with one inch of boiling water. Reduce the heat and cover. Steam until the vegetables are crisp. When steaming buns, add large amounts of water and cook over high heat to produce enough steam — the buns will taste better. The amount of heat and water will depend on the type of food being cooked.

Cookware

The best cookware is made from glass, ceramic, or lead-free earthenware. These do not leach metals or other ingredients into the food. Heavy stainless steel is also a good choice for healthy cooking, because it is the most inert metal. Porcelain-coated cookware is non-reactive and conducts heat well, but once it chips, food is exposed to toxins. Avoid cooking with aluminum and aluminum foil, Teflon, and poor-quality stainless steel. These leach harmful toxins into the food, both raw and cooked.

To avoid a metallic taste, remove food immediately after cooking and do not store in metal containers.

E. Getting Ready to Cook

Confucius once said: "Do not eat food that looks bad. Do not eat food that smells bad. Do not eat at the wrong time." Do we think about why we eat? How we select our food?

1. COOKING FOR DIFFERENT TEMPERAMENTS AND HEALTH CONDITIONS

At different ages people have different dispositions and health conditions. Balancing the relaxing and energizing qualities of food can attune one to the cycles of nature and spark positive changes for a more fulfilled life. Cooking with a proper attitude is as important as the quality of the food and the cooking method. The appearance, taste, balance, and presentation of the food (and the way everyone feels after eating it) are reflections of the cook's physical, mental, emotional and spiritual state. There is an invisible energy conveyed by the cook that affects the food and everyone who consumes it. When preparing food, be mindful of what you wish to accomplish.

For a lighter taste, cook food quickly with little or no salt. The food will have an activating yet relaxing quality, and is suitable for stagnant and tense people, and for children who are naturally active and joyful with a fast metabolism. It stimulates their mental and emotional growth.

For a more harmonious and sweeter taste, cook food on a low heat for a longer time, without disturbing it. The food will have a patient quality and can calm an angry person.

For heartier and more strengthening food, add a bit more salt and oil and cook with pressure. This is best for people who are inactive or weak, or who are depressed, need more human warmth, and need a variety of interesting food.

Activities such as tossing, mashing, pureeing, stirring, and kneading help to blend and energize the food. They stimulate a weak digestive system and add spirit and joy to one's life.

For a varied and balanced diet, use a combination of the above methods, balancing the relaxing and energizing qualities of the food. Adapt them to the seasons and needs of those for whom you are cooking.

2. COLORS, SHAPES, FLAVORS, AROMA, AND THE NATURE OF FOOD

Allow the colors, shapes, tastes, aroma and nature of the vegetables to be your guide in shaping a meal. Use simple combinations. Mixing too many things together usually results in confusing tastes for the taste buds and the digestive system. Notice your own state of mind after such meals.

Colors: Red in tomatoes supports a healthy heart; orange in carrots enhances good vision; yellow in corn promotes smooth skin; green in kale prevents colon cancer; blue

in blueberries fights inflammation; purple in plums is anti-aging; white in turnip aids the lungs; black in mushrooms boosts the immune system; the brown in rice hulls and potato skins is an antioxidant.

Shapes: Cut vegetables in different shapes such as: julienne, half-moons, triangles, flowers, diagonal cuts, large diagonal wedges, blocks, squares, rounds. Each shape will have a different taste and will require a different method of cooking. Vegetables that are cooked together should roughly be the same size.

Flavors: Chinese medicine classifies the flavor of food into five categories: sour (vinegar), sweet (apple), bitter (tomato), pungent (ginger) and salty (soy sauce). Different tastes strengthen different organs. Adjust the taste. Add a little less or a little more salt, sweetener, soy sauce, or vinegar.

Aroma: The unique aroma of Chinese cooking is attributed to sesame oil, star anise, peppercorns, 5-spice powder, celery, seaweed and fermented black beans. Use delicately and create variety.

The Nature of Food: Understanding the nature of each vegetable is fundamental in creating a balance in each dish. In Chinese medicine, a vegetable can be cold or warm in nature. For example, when cooking vegetables with a cold nature, like Chinese cabbage, cook it with dried shitake mushrooms or ginger to neutralize the coldness.

3. VEGETABLES IN SEASON

Winter and Spring

- **Root vegetables and tubers:** Daikon, carrots, potatoes, yams, burdock, kohlrabi

- **Vegetables with heads:** Cabbage, napa cabbage, iceberg lettuce, cauliflower, broccoli, Brussels sprouts

- **Leafy greens:** Mustard, Chinese cabbage, asparagus, Shanghai bok choy, spinach, pea pods, cabbage, leafy lettuces, yam leaves, celery, beet greens

Summer and Fall

- **Rhizomes:** Lotus root, lotus seed, an assortment of bamboo, taro, fresh young ginger, aged ginger

- **Melons:** Luffa, winter melons, bitter melons, cucumbers, Japanese cucumbers, pumpkins

- **Leafy greens:** kale, collards, chard

- **Legumes:** String beans, long beans, mung beans, red beans, peanuts, sweet peas, snow peas

All Four Seasons

Mung bean sprouts, soybean sprouts, yam leaves, mushrooms, cloud ears (edible fungus), seaweed, seaweed sprouts

4. PREPARING RHIZOMES, TUBERS, AND MELONS

- **Daikon, Carrot, Burdock:** Eaten raw or cooked, with or without peels.
- **Cucumber:** Eaten raw or cooked, with or without peels. Remove hard seed.
- **Japanese Cucumber:** Eaten raw, cooked or pickled, with or without peels.
- **Potatoes and Yams:** May be cooked, with or without peels.
- **Bamboo, Taro, Bottle Gourd, Luffa:** Peeled and cooked.
- **Bitter Melon:** Eaten raw or cooked, with or without peels. Seeds are not eaten.
- **Winter Melon:** Peeled, seeded and cooked.
- **Kohlrabi:** Eaten raw or cooked, peeled.
- **Lotus Root:** Cooked or blanched, with or without peels.
- **Lotus Seeds:** Cooked, with peels.
- **Chinese Cabbage:** Cooked.
- **Fresh Young Ginger:** Not peeled.
- **Aged Ginger:** Peeled.
- **Pumpkin:** Cooked, but it is not necessary to peel or remove the seed.

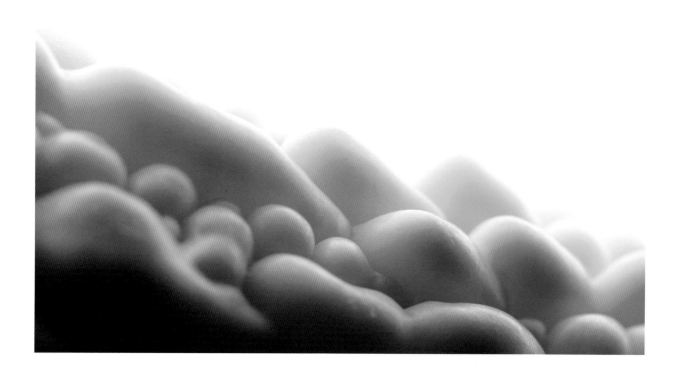

5. WASHING VEGETABLES

The main concern is to wash away as many pesticides as possible, especially on fruit. In Taiwan, due to the long-term use of pesticides, health problems related to poison are becoming more severe. Below are three ways to wash vegetables:

- Soak produce in a solution of apple cider vinegar for five minutes. Use one tablespoon vinegar per gallon of soak water.

- Add a few drops of natural detergent in water to cover produce. Soak for five minutes and rinse well.

- Hydrogen peroxide is also effective and pure. Add ½ teaspoon to one gallon of water and soak produce ten minutes.

In general, wash vegetables three times in large quantities of clean water. Drain and save the water for later use. Use a soft-bristled brush to clean areas where dirt and pesticides may lodge, or cut the areas out. Trim the roots of leafy vegetables and compost the outermost leaves. Separate the rest of the leaves and wash. Wash the roots and tubers before peeling them. Cabbage does not harbor parasites that infest humans.

Tips

To conserve freshness, leave vegetables and hearty greens outside for a day before washing. If they begin to dry, soak them in cool water before using.

Whether a beginner or experienced cook, be simple and have a beginner's mind. Use your creativity and trust yourself to cook well. The results will be much better than expected. So roll up your sleeves, put on an apron, turn the page, and start cooking.

FOODS TO
PREPARE
AHEAD FOR
CHINESE
DISHES

A. Four Variations of Vegetable Broth

Homemade vegetable broth has its own natural sweet and/or tart flavor. It will make any dish tastier. There is no need to add sugar, MSG, or other artificial seasoning.

Variation One: Mushrooms, Kombu Seaweed, Sugar Cane, Soybean Sprouts, Carrots

Makes 12 to 14 cups

Ingredients

3 dried shitaki mushrooms

12 inches (30 cm) kombu seaweed*

12 inches (30 cm) sugar cane, peeled and cut into 2-inch (5 cm) pieces

1¼ pounds (20 oz/600 g) soybean sprouts

1 carrot, chopped

10 cups (2½ quarts/liters) cold filtered water

* Do not wipe the kombu prior to use as the white powder adds flavor. Remove dirt if you see any.

Directions

- Soak the mushrooms in hot water for twenty minutes, until soft. Rinse well to remove grit and squeeze out the water. Trim the stems and cut the mushrooms into quarters.
- Soak the kombu in cold water for twenty minutes, until tender enough to cut. Drain well. Cut into 2-inch (5 cm) wide pieces.
- Place all ingredients in a large pot and add enough water to cover well.
- Bring to a boil. Reduce the heat to low. Cover and simmer about fifty to sixty minutes.
- Strain and use immediately in a recipe or freeze batches up to one month. Thaw well and use as needed.

Variation Two: Kombu Seaweed and Kohlrabi

Makes 12 cups

Ingredients

12 inches (30 cm) *kombu seaweed

1 kohlrabi, peeled and cut into chunks

10 cups (2½ quarts/liters) cold water

_____

*Do not wipe the kombu prior to use as the white powder adds flavor. Remove dirt if you see any.

Directions

- Soak the kombu in cold water for twenty minutes, until tender enough to cut. Drain well. Cut into 2-inch (5 cm) wide pieces.

- Place all ingredients in a large pot and cover well with water. Bring to a boil. Reduce the heat to low. Cover and simmer about fifty to sixty minutes.

- Strain and use immediately or freeze batches up to one month. Thaw well and use as needed.

Variation Three: Dried Shitake Mushrooms and Daikon Radish

Makes 10 to 12 cups

Ingredients

5 dried shitake mushrooms

1 daikon radish or turnip, peeled and chopped

10 cups (2 ½ quarts/liters) cold filtered water

Directions

- Soak the mushrooms in hot water for twenty minutes, until soft. Rinse well to remove grit and squeeze out the water. Trim the stems and cut the mushrooms into halves.
- Place all ingredients in a large pot and cover well with water. Bring to a boil.
- Reduce the heat to low. Cover and simmer about fifty to sixty minutes.
- Strain and use immediately or freeze batches up to one month. Thaw and use as needed.

Variation Four: Kombu Seaweed, Sugar Cane, Soybean Sprouts, Carrot, Cabbage

Makes 12 to 14 cups

Ingredients

12 inches (30 cm) kombu seaweed*

12 inches (30 cm) sugar cane, peeled and cut into 2-inch (5 cm) pieces

1 ¼ pounds (20 oz/550 g) soybean sprouts

1 carrot, chopped

1 head cabbage, chopped

10 cups (2 ½ quarts/liters) cold water

---

*Do not wipe the kombu prior to use as the white powder adds flavor. Remove dirt if you see any.

Directions

- Soak the kombu in cold water for twenty minutes, until tender enough to cut. Drain well. Cut into 2-inch (5 cm) wide pieces.
- Place all ingredients in a large pot and cover well with water. Bring to a boil. Reduce the heat to low. Cover and simmer about fifty to sixty minutes.
- Strain and use immediately or freeze batches up to one month. Thaw well and use as needed.

B. Tofu Pouches, Wheat Gluten, Bean Sprouts, and More

1. TOFU, MUSHROOMS, AND CHICK PEAS
WITH SWEET BLACK BEAN SAUCE

Makes 16 servings

Tofu mushroom relish is a flavor enhancer that can be served with noodles, rice or vegetable dishes.

Ingredients

5 dried shitake mushrooms

5 blocks pressed tofu (12–14 oz/340–450 g per block), flavored with Chinese 5-spice powder

2 cups (16 oz/440 g) cooked or canned chick peas (garbanzo beans)

1 cup (5 oz/160 g) wheat germ

1 cup (6 oz/180 g) all-purpose whole wheat flour

1 tablespoon sesame oil

Sauce

1 cup (8 fl oz/250 ml) soy sauce

2 cups miso (or black bean sauce)

½ cup (4 oz/115 g) brown sugar or equivalent sweetener

Directions

- Soak the mushrooms in hot water for twenty minutes, until soft. Rinse well to remove grit and squeeze out the water. Trim the stems and cut the mushrooms into halves.

- While the mushrooms are soaking, combine sauce ingredients in a separate bowl.

- Rinse the tofu and dice.

- Grind the wheat germ and flour together in a blender or with mortar and pestle. Dry-roast in a skillet until brown and aromatic.

- Heat a wok or skillet over medium-high heat. Add the oil. Just before it begins to smoke, add the diced tofu and stir-fry until golden brown, about two minutes.

- Add the mushrooms and stir-fry until soft, about three minutes.

- Add the garbanzo beans and wheat germ mixture. Continue to stir.

- Add the sauce and enough water to cover. Reduce heat to low. Cover and simmer for thirty minutes.

- Serve immediately or freeze in batches for up to one month. Thaw well and use as needed.

NOTE: For a healthier dish, the ingredients can be stir-fried with water.

2. TOFU POUCHES

The Japanese were the first to develop tofu pouches. They are made by cutting sheets of dried tofu into thin slices and deep frying them until they puff up like a pouch.

Nori Tofu-Pouch Rolls with Dried Bean Curd

Nori tofu-pouch rolls are the main ingredient in sweet and sour dishes. They are added to other stir-fried dishes and can be served for everyday and special occasions. Nori is a Japanese seaweed that is pressed into sheets.

Ingredients

1 ⅓ pounds (600 g) thick tofu pouches

2 sheets nori

1 sheet dried bean curd

1 tablespoon whole grain flour and 1 tablespoon water, mixed together

Seasoned Mixture

1 tablespoon soy sauce

½ teaspoon pepper

1 tablespoon sesame oil

½ teaspoon sweetener

½ teaspoon salt

Directions

- Combine ingredients for the sauce and set aside.
- Tear tofu-pouches into small pieces. Mix with seasoned mixture.
- Cut dried bean curd into two small sheets.
- Place one sheet of nori between the two sheets of bean curd.
- Spread half of the seasoned tofu pouches on top of the nori sheet.
- Roll up like a spring roll. Seal ends with flour mixture. (Repeat the same steps for all rolls).
- Steam for twenty minutes on low heat. Cool and freeze for up to a month. Thaw and use as needed.

Tip

To help the rolls keep their shape and not break apart, squeeze tightly while rolling up. Cook on low heat and cool the rolls completely before handling them.

Fried Tofu Pouches

Tofu pouches can be stuffed with rice for sushi or added to fried noodles and stir-fried vegetable dishes.

Ingredients

Tofu pouches and oil for frying

Directions

- Cut the tofu pouches into desired shapes. Fry in batches for one to two minutes, until golden. Drain on absorbent towels.
- Serve immediately or freeze for up to one month. Thaw and use as needed.

3. KONNYAKU (JAPANESE YAM CAKES)

Konnyaku comes in a powder that is made from a root much like the yam.

Makes 4 to 6 servings

Ingredients

¼ teaspoon alkali powder
(potassium bicarbonate)

1 ½ cups (12 fl oz/350 ml) water

2 tablespoons white konnyaku
powder

1 tablespoon rice vinegar

1 teaspoon salt

Directions

- Dissolve the alkali powder in the water. Slowly add the konnyaku powder. Mix well with chopsticks until the mixture reaches a thick consistency. Pour onto a large plate. Hold the plate up and shake it to prevent air bubbles and to distribute the mixture evenly.

- Leave at room temperature for two hours until the konnyaku sets, or steam for thirty minutes on low heat.

- Cut into any size or shape that you prefer. Place in a pot and cover with fresh water.

- Add the rice vinegar and salt. Bring to a boil. Reduce the heat to low. Cover and simmer for thirty minutes.

- Serve immediately or store in refrigerator for up to one week.

4. EASY RISING DOUGH

Makes approximately 12 buns or dumplings

The dough can be used to make vegetable-stuffed buns, multi-grain buns, sweet buns, dumplings and more.

Tip

Stir in the same direction to prevent air pouches. Cook on low heat for a smoother texture.

Ingredients

2 cups (10 oz/300 g) whole wheat flour

2 cups (10 oz/300 g) medium gluten flour

1 tablespoon brown sugar

½ teaspoon salt

Directions

- 1 tablespoon yeast, dissolved in 2 ½ cups (22 fl oz/650 ml) lukewarm water

- Using a pair of chopsticks or a fork, in a large bowl, combine the whole wheat and gluten flour with the brown sugar and salt. Mix well and make a big hole in the center of the flour mixture.

Picture 1: Slowly pour the yeast mixture into the hole.

Picture 2-1: Use chopsticks to mix yeast into about two thirds of the flour, to make dough.

Picture 2-2: Cover the dough with a lid or wet towel. Wait for it to double in size.

Picture 3: Knead in the rest of the flour until the surface is smooth.

Picture 4: Cover the dough again with a lid or a wet towel. Wait for it to double in size. Shape the dough into buns or make dumplings.

Tip

This method not only makes the dough rise faster, but gives it a smooth, elastic texture. The buns will be soft and chewy.

5. RED BEAN PASTE

Use as a filling for sweet steamed buns or in other desserts.

Makes 5 to 6 cups

Ingredients

3 cups (20 oz/600 g) aduki beans, soaked six to eight hours and drained
1 ½ cups (10 oz/300 g) rock candy or equivalent sweetener

Directions

- Place the beans in a large pot with two parts fresh water. Bring to a boil over high heat. Reduce the heat to low. Cover and cook for one hour, or until soft.
- Transfer the beans and liquid to a skillet.
- Add the rock candy and stir continuously until melted, simultaneously mashing the beans into a paste until all the liquid has evaporated.
- Serve immediately or divide into small portions and freeze up to one month. Thaw and use as needed.

Variation

Try different kinds of beans to see which you like best. All beans must be completely cooked, or the paste will be grainy. Mung beans tend to be too grainy and coarse.

Information

Aduki Beans: Chinese medicine considers aduki beans to have a moderate nature and a sweet-and-sour flavor. They influence the heart and small intestines, strengthen the kidneys, detoxify the body, remove heat conditions, promote weight loss and increase mother's milk. To tonify the kidneys, take ½ cup bean broth 30 minutes before meals.

6. HOW TO MAKE SOYBEAN SPROUTS

⅓ cup soybeans makes 1 cup sprouts

Directions

- Place soybeans in a bowl and cover well with water. Soak for six to eight hours or overnight.

- Drain well and place in a dry container lined with kitchen paper or a cloth to absorb the moisture. Cover and place a weight on top for pressure (a couple cans of soda). Let stand in a dry place for two or three days.

- Check every day to see if they are sprouting correctly. The sprouts are ready when they are around two inches (5 cm) long.

- Remove the skins and trim the roots, using scissors (optional). Rinse with a little water before using.

7. HOW TO MAKE MUNG BEAN SPROUTS

⅓ cup beans makes 1 cup sprouts

Method One

- Pick and clean the mung beans well. Rinse in water three to four times.
- Place the mung beans in a bowl. Add enough water to cover well. Cover the bowl with a lid and soak the beans six to eight hours or overnight.
- Drain well. Cover and place the bowl away from sunlight at room temperature for two days. After two days you will see beautiful sprouts appearing.

Method Two

- Soak the beans six to eight hours or overnight. Drain well.
- Wet a clean cloth or kitchen napkin and squeeze out the excess water. Wrap the mung beans tightly in the damp cloth and place in a covered container for one to two days, out of sunlight.
- After one day, small sprouts will appear. For longer sprouts, keep for one more day. Sprouts will stay fresh in the fridge for two to three days.

Other Methods

Sprouting Jar: Cover with a sprouting lid. Tilt the jar at a 45-degree angle, lid facing down. This allows airflow and adequate drainage.

Sprouting Bag: Hang in a cool, well-ventilated place, out of sunlight.

Bamboo Steamer: Excellent drainage. Rinse and drain the sprouts every eight to twelve hours, for two to three days, until sprouts reach the desired size.

This offering of the faithful is the fruit of work and care,
I reflect upon my conduct, have I truly earned my share.
Of the poisons of the mind, the most destructive one is greed
As medicine cures illness, I take only what I need
To sustain my cultivation and to realize the Way,
So we contemplate in silence on these offerings today.
    —*The Five Contemplations When Eating*, instructions of the Buddha

RECIPES

A. Appetizers and Condiments

The tongue is forerunner to the stomach.
If your appetite is healthy,
  your stomach is healthy.
A healthy stomach absorbs nutrients,
Welcoming a happy future.
  —Dharma Realm Cookbook Team

Bon Appétit!

1. Sweet and Sour Pickled Vegetables

Makes 5 to 6 cups

Ingredients

1 turnip, cut into ½-inch (1.3 cm) cubes

2 Japanese cucumbers, cut into ½-inch (1.3 cm) cubes

1 cup (120 g) fresh young ginger, sliced

1 tablespoon salt

1 cup (7 oz/200 g) rock candy or equivalent sweetener

1 cup (8 fl oz/250 ml) lemon juice

Directions

- Make sure that the cutting board, chopsticks, juicer and containers are clean and dry when making pickled vegetables. Water and dirt can contaminate them and ruin the taste.
- Combine the turnips and cucumbers with the salt and ginger slices. Place in a ceramic or glass container. Seal and marinate until soft, about two weeks in a cool place.
- Rinse with cold water and drain well. Add the rock candy and lemon juice. Marinate for one day longer.

Variation

Use bok choy, cabbage, watercress, carrots, lotus root, cauliflower or eggplant instead of turnips. They all make delicious preserved vegetables.

Information

Pickled Vegetables: When sealed tightly, pickled vegetables ferment naturally and produce healthy lactobacillus, which are responsible for the sour taste and delicious aroma. They are highly nutritious and improve the intestinal flora essential for proper digestion and elimination. They are also a good source of B vitamins for vegetarians.

We should be true in everything we do.
We should be honest in everything we say.
We should cherish our food and not let it spoil and go to waste.
If we are not careful in this, our blessings will run out.
We will lose more than we will gain.

    —Venerable Master Hsuan Hua (1918–1995)

2. Miso Kohlrabi with Apple

Makes 3 to 4 servings

Ingredients

1 kohlrabi, peeled and cut into ½-inch (1.3 cm) pieces

1 apple, unpeeled, cored and sliced

Sauce

½ cup organic miso

½ teaspoon sugar or equivalent sweetener

1 cup (8 fl oz/250 ml) grapefruit juice

Directions

- Make sure that the cutting board, chopsticks, juicer and containers are clean and dry when making pickled vegetables. Water and dirt can contaminate them and ruin the taste.
- In a mixing bowl, combine the ingredients for the sauce and mix with the kohlrabi and apple slices. Cover and marinate for one hour to allow the flavors to blend.
- Turn ingredients at least once during the marinating process.
- Use immediately or store in a glass or ceramic container in the refrigerator for up to one week.

Information

Miso Kohlrabi: Famous in Japanese soups and in rice congee with bok choy. Gourmet food lover and scholar Su Dongpoh of the Northern Sung Dynasty invented the famous "Dongpoh Broth" made with miso kohlrabi.

Lotus flowers and leaves fill the pond.
The blossoms are fragrant, so is the water,
When the girls gather flowers, they don't pick them all;
They leave a few to shade the ducks and drakes who live below.

—Wang Shu (Qing Dynasty, 1644–1912) from Kindness

3. Shredded Seaweed Salad with Japanese Cucumbers

Makes 4 to 6 servings

Ingredients

1½ pounds (10 oz/300 g) raw shredded kelp or kombu seaweed (see page 10)
2 Japanese cucumbers, julienned
Shredded carrot for color

Marinade

1 tablespoon light soy sauce
¼ tablespoon sesame oil
1 tablespoon sugar or equivalent sweetener
1 tablespoon lemon juice
2 tablespoons fresh young ginger, shredded
1 tablespoon dark vinegar

Directions

- Rinse and blanch the shredded kelp.
- Combine the ingredients for marinade and mix with the shredded kelp. Set aside.
- Before serving, toss in the cucumbers and shredded carrot. Mix well and transfer to a serving dish. Serve cold.

Tip

Add vinegar to seaweed during blanching to soften it and to eliminate any aftertaste.

Information

Kombu and Kelp: Seaweed from the same family. They have a cooling nature and salty flavor; provide a wealth of minerals, vitamins, and amino acids; and are an excellent source of protein, iodine, calcium and iron. They alkalize the blood and soften masses in the body such as tumors and goiters, aid hearing, remove residues of radiation from the body, treat cancer, and are useful in weight loss.

*The meaning of rescuing and setting animals free is to give those
facing the imminent threat of death a chance to live.*
—Venerable Master Hsuan Hua (1918–1995)

4. Fragrant Peanuts

Makes 4 to 6 servings

Ingredients

1 tablespoon oil

2 ½ pounds (20 oz/600 g) raw shelled peanuts, with skins

2 cups (500 g) salt

Directions

- Rinse and drain the peanuts thoroughly.
- In a skillet heat the oil and sauté the peanuts with salt. Using a wooden spoon, stir the peanuts constantly until the color changes, and they make a crackling sound. It will become easier to stir.
- Immediately remove the peanuts, place them in a strainer, and shake out as much salt as desired.

Tip

Use low heat to prevent scorching. It is best to eat the whole peanut, including the skin, which is nutritious.

Variation

Drain them slightly after rinsing and sauté right away. The flavor of the salt will easily seep into the peanuts when moist.

Information

Peanuts: Known in China as the "longevity nut," peanuts are highly nutritious and easily absorbed by the body. Chinese medicine considers them to have a warming nature and sweet flavor. They affect the lungs, stomach and spleen-pancreas; lubricate the intestines, break up phlegm and stop bleeding. Raw peanuts treat deafness and peanut shell tea lowers blood pressure.

Caution

Peanuts can cause skin outbreaks and slow down the metabolic rate of the liver. People who are sluggish, overweight, and cancerous should avoid them. They are often sprayed heavily with chemicals and grown on land saturated with synthetic fertilizers. Peanuts are also subject to the aflatoxin fungus and may promote cancer. It is best to eat only organic peanuts.

Do not say that a life of an insect is small,
And not rescue it when it's drowning;
One must know that innate compassion
Is the heart of goodness.
　　—Great Master Hong Yi (1879–1942) from Kindness

5. Stir-Fried Turnip with Tofu and Five-Spice Powder

Makes 4 to 6 servings

Ingredients

1 cup minced preserved turnips

1 extra firm tofu (14 oz/397 g)

Oil for stir-fry

½ teaspoon sugar or equivalent sweetener

1 tablespoon soy sauce

1 teaspoon five-spice powder

Directions

- Rinse the tofu and drain well. Squeeze completely dry to retain flavor, then crumble. Drain again.
- Heat a wok or skillet over medium-high heat. Add the oil. Just before it begins to smoke, add the turnips and tofu. Stir-fry about two to three minutes, or until aromatic.
- Add the sweetener, soy sauce and five-spice powder. Continue stirring until all ingredients are thoroughly mixed.
- Transfer to a serving dish and serve immediately.

Variation

Use diced celery and carrots instead of turnips.

Information

Turnips: Chinese medicine considers the turnip to have a neutral thermal nature and a pungent, sweet and bitter flavor. It improves the circulation of *qi* (energy), builds the blood, promotes sweating, aids in absorbing nutrients, relieves coughing, improves appetite and detoxifies the body. The turnip prevents heart attack and is helpful for diabetes, indigestion, lung congestion, asthma, and sinus problems. Turnip greens are especially rich in vitamin A and C. A Chinese proverb proclaims, "When turnips are in the markets, doctors have nothing to do."

Five-Spice Powder: A mixture of fennel, anise, cinnamon bark, cloves and Szechuan pepper. It is very pungent, so use sparingly.

> *I am a great eater of beef, and I believe that does harm to my wit.*
>
> — Sir Andre Augcheet, from the play, *Twelfth Night* by William Shakespeare (1566–1616)

Sickness enters the mouth,
Calamity comes out of the mouth.
   —Venerable Master Hsuan Hua (1918–1995)

6. Nostalgic Fermented Black Soybeans with Ginger

Makes 4 to 6 servings

Ingredients

2 cups (15 oz/425 g) fermented black beans, rinsed and drained

½ tablespoon oil for stir-fry

1 tablespoon ginger, grated

½ tablespoon sugar or equivalent sweetener

Directions

- Heat a wok or skillet over medium-high heat. Add the oil. Just before it begins to smoke, add the ginger and stir-fry for one to two minutes, or until aromatic.
- Stir in the beans and add the sweetener. Continue stir-frying until all ingredients are thoroughly mixed. Transfer to a warm serving dish and serve as a condiment.

Variation

Add bits of dried daikon, turnip or tofu, or combinations.

Information

Fermented Black Soybeans: Japanese scientists say, "Eating fermented black beans can prevent food poisoning and intestinal diseases." The beans also aid digestion, delay aging, increase brain power, enhance liver function, prevent hypertension and cancer, and eliminate fatigue.

Caution

Fermented black beans are high in salt and should be consumed sparingly.

The love for all living creatures is the most noble attribute of man.
— Charles Darwin, English naturalist (1809–1882)

7. Salty Peanuts with Anise Stars

Makes 4 to 6 servings

Ingredients

1 ½ cups (10 oz/300 g) raw peanuts, with skins

3 anise stars

1 tablespoon lemon juice

2 tablespoons soy sauce

Directions

- Rinse the peanuts. Add two parts water to one part peanuts in a medium pot. Bring to a boil and cover. Remove from stove and drain.
- Add another round of water, along with anise, lemon juice and soy sauce.
- Bring to a boil. Reduce to low heat. Simmer until the peanuts are fully cooked, about one hour. If you prefer a saltier flavor, add a little salt at the end of cooking.
- Transfer to a warm serving dish and serve immediately.

Tip

Do not add salt to peanuts until they are soft and completely cooked, or they will be hard. Test peanuts for softness by pinching.

I think a vegetarian's attitude towards life starts with the simple wish for physiological balance. Thus, it is beneficial to the ideals of humanity.

— Albert Einstein, Nobel Prize winner in physics (1879–1936)

8. Purple Laver Seaweed Paté

Makes 4 to 6 servings

Ingredients
1 sheet of purple laver seaweed
Sprinkling of sesame seeds
1 tablespoon soy sauce
1 tablespoon sugar or equivalent sweetener
1 tablespoon rice vinegar

Directions
- Cut the laver into ½-inch (2 cm) wide pieces and rinse. Blanch and drain well.
- Add the soy sauce, sweetener and vinegar. Mix well and sprinkle with the sesame seeds.
- Transfer to a warm serving dish and serve immediately.

Variation
Substitute laver with nori seaweed.

Tip
If the laver is not drained well, the flavor will be diluted.

Information
Purple Laver: Edible purple seaweed that comes pressed into sheets. It has a high content of dietary minerals, particularly iodine and iron. It is predominantly consumed in East Asia and also in Wales, where it is used for making laver bread.

The obligations of law and equity reach only to mankind; but kindness and beneficence should be extended to the creatures of every species and these will flow from the breast of a true man, as streams that issue from the living fountain.

— Plutarch, Greek biographer and moralist (46–120 A.D.)

9. Traditional Pickled Mustard Greens with Red Hot Peppers

Makes 4 to 6 servings

Ingredients

1 ½ pounds (20 oz/600 g) pickled mustard greens, rinsed and cubed

1–2 tablespoons oil for sauté

2 red hot peppers, diced

Dash of light soy sauce and a dash of sugar or equivalent sweetener

Directions

- Heat the oil in a skillet and sauté the peppers for one to two minutes.
- Stir in the soy sauce and bring to a boil.
- Add the pickled mustard greens and sweetener, stirring constantly to mix well.
- Reduce to low heat and simmer until the water is completely evaporated.
- Transfer to a warm serving dish and serve immediately

Tip

To seal in the flavors, allow the water to evaporate.

Information

Pickled mustard: Can increase the appetite, aid in digestion, and facilitate the absorption of iron. Fresh vegetables, which contain vitamin C, should be eaten along with pickled mustard. The combination of vitamin C and sea salt restore and prevent cancer.

Caution

Pickled mustard with a funky taste or that contains mold can be carcinogenic and should not be eaten.

Animals are my friends, and I don't eat my friends.
—George Bernard Shaw, Irish playwright (1856–1950)

10. Coral Seaweed Salad with Japanese Cucumbers

Makes 4 to 6 servings

Ingredients

1 cup (37.5 g) coral seaweed

3 Japanese cucumbers, julienned

Juice of 1 lemon

1 tablespoon salt

1 cup (120 g) fresh young ginger, julienned

½ cup (12 g) red hot peppers, julienned

Drizzle of sesame oil

Directions

- Rinse the coral seaweed and soak in cold water overnight. Change the water once or twice during soak time. Drain and cut into small pieces. Set aside.
- Rub salt into cucumbers and marinate for ten minutes. Rinse and drain well.
- Mix the coral and marinated cucumbers together. Add the lemon juice, salt, ginger and hot peppers. Toss well and drizzle the sesame oil on top for a glossy sheen.

Tips

Adding lemon juice to cucumbers just before serving will render them a bright emerald green.

Coral seaweed will become sticky if heated or left in a warm environment.

Information

Coral Seaweed: Looks somewhat like coral, and is sometimes called Sea Bird Nest. It is rich in enzymes, nutrients, minerals, calcium, iron, fiber and protein, and is especially good for the skin and hair. It is best when fresh, but can also be found packaged in Asian markets or ordered online.

Not caging birds in this life, we will not be put in jail in future lives;
Not fishing in this life, we will not become beggars in future lives;
Not taking lives in this life, we will not encounter difficulties in future lives.
   —Venerable Master Hsuan Hua (1918–1995)

11. Pressed Tofu with Red and Green Bell Peppers

Makes 4 to 6 servings

Ingredients

10 ounces (300 g) pressed tofu

1 cup (4 oz/115 g) green bell peppers, cut into diagonal pieces ¼-inch wide

½ cup (4 oz/106 g) fermented black beans, rinsed and drained

1 tablespoon oil for stir-fry

½ red hot pepper, julienned

1 tablespoon ginger, grated

1 tablespoon soy sauce

Directions

- Rinse and shred the dry tofu into strips. Set aside.
- Heat a wok or skillet over medium-high heat. Add the oil. Just before it begins to smoke, add the ginger and stir-fry about two minutes, or until aromatic. Stir in the beans and stir-fry for one to two more minutes.
- Add the tofu and green peppers. Stir-fry for two minutes until the peppers are almost done, but still bright green.
- Add the soy sauce and red hot peppers. Toss briefly to thoroughly mix the ingredients.
- Transfer to a warm serving dish and serve immediately.

Once people spend time with farm animals in a loving way — a pig or cow or a little chicken or a turkey — they might find they relate with them the same way they relate with dogs and cats. People don't really think of them that way because they're on the plate. Why should they be food when other animals are pets? I would never eat my doggies.

— Alicia Silverstone, actress, author of The Kind Diet (1976–　　)

12. Cellophane Noodle Salad with Ginger Sauce

Makes 4 to 6 servings

Ingredients

2 bundles of cellophane noodles (shaped like vermicelli)

½ cup carrots, julienned

1 cup (7 oz/200 g) Japanese cucumber, julienned

Ginger Sauce

½ cup ginger, julienned

1 tablespoon soy sauce paste

½ tablespoon sugar

1 tablespoon rice vinegar

Toasted sesame oil

Directions

- Rinse and blanch the cellophane noodles. Set aside.
- Combine the ingredients for the ginger sauce. Set aside.
- Before serving, mix the noodles, carrots and cucumbers together.
- Toss with the ginger sauce and transfer to a serving dish. Serve cold.

Information

Cellophane Noodles: The Chinese started making cellophane noodles from mung beans over 300 years ago in the Shangdong Province. The best quality noodles come from a port called Lung Ko, Dragon Mouth, thus the name Lungko Cellophane Noodles. Foreigners often call these cellophane noodles "Chinese Glass Noodles" or "Spring Rain Noodles."

Children who grow up getting nutrition from plant foods rather than meats have a tremendous health advantage. They are less likely to develop weight problems, diabetes, high blood pressure and some forms of cancer.
— Dr. Benjamin Spock, pediatrician, author (1903–1998)

13. Miso Turnips

Ingredients

13 pounds (6 kg) unpeeled turnips, cut
  into 1¼-inch (3 cm) cubes

2¼ cups (10 oz/300 g) salt

Miso Marinade

2 cups (18 oz/500 g) red sugar or equivalent sweetener

1 tablespoon water

2¼ cups (10 oz/300 g) miso

2 cups (16 fl oz/473 ml) water

Directions

- Add the salt to the turnips and knead until the salt is absorbed. Place in a glass or ceramic bowl and lay a heavy weight on top for twenty-four hours.
- Knead two to three times during this time, so the salty flavor will seep in.
- Rinse the turnips well and squeeze out the water and salt.
- Place in a cheesecloth or bag. Put the weight back on top for another day to drain out the excess water.

How to Make the Marinade

Combine the sweetener and one tablespoon water in a saucepan and cook on low heat until dissolved. Add the miso and two cups of water. Bring to just below a boil. Remove from the heat and cool. Pour the miso marinade over the turnips and mix well.

Divide the turnips into portions and store in glass or ceramic jars. Cover with lids and place in refrigerator. Marinate for three days. They will keep up to three months.

Variation

Make soy turnips: Substitute the miso with two cups of soy sauce and two cups of white vinegar. The turnips will keep longer because the vinegar acts as a preservative.

Tip

Marinating with salt and pressing out all the water helps the turnips to keep longer. Use only boiled water, or the turnips tend to grow mold.

The Buddha considers all creatures as if his sons.
Saving one creature is like saving the Buddha's son,
Making all Buddhas happy.
　—Great Master Yin Guang (1861–1940)

14. Preserved Yellow Plums

Ingredients

8 ounces (225 g) fresh or dried astragalus herb

26 ½ pounds (12 kg) green plums, blemish free

4 ½ pounds (2 kg) coarse salt, non-iodized

4 ½ pounds (2 kg) sugar or equivalent sweetener

11 pounds (5 kg) rock sugar

Note

The large amounts of salt and sugar are for preserving the plums and can be well drained.

Directions

- Remove the tiny black stems from the plums, using a toothpick.

- Dry the plums on a flat basket in the sun or on a baking sheet in the oven on low heat, until the plums are dry.

- Place the plums in a large, wide-mouth, deep container made of ceramic or glass that has been sterilized. Add salt directly to the plums (no need to rinse them) and mix well. Place a sterilized wooden lid or plate on top of the plums and a sterilized weight on the lid.

- After three days, squeeze the clear liquid out of the plums and scrub and clean them with your hands (a sterilization effect). Drain well.

- When the plums are dried well, add the sugar and follow the same steps above: Cover with a sterilized lid or plate and place a weight on top for three more days.

- Add a layer of plums, then a layer of the astragalus herb with leaves and stems. Top each layer with rock candy. Repeat until the jar is about eighty percent full. The astragalus will turn the plums bright yellow.

- Cover the container with thin paper and tie a string around it to make it airtight. Leave it in a cool, dark place.

- Every two months, for the next six months, add another layer of rock candy on top. The preserved plums will be ready after six months.

Tip

Do not rinse the plums or mold will develop.

Information

Plums: Slightly cooling in nature with a sweet-and-sour flavor; contain protein, carbohydrates and sixteen amino acids that are essential to the human body. They have a blood cleansing property and are used to treat stomach problems and liver diseases such as diabetes and cirrhosis. Plums prevent heat stroke, relieve fatigue, calm the spirit, eliminate heat, and aid digestion. Stewed plums are a traditional remedy for constipation.

Caution

People with delicate digestion or ulcers should avoid plums.

Astragalus (Huang Qi): Used medicinally by Chinese herbalists, and also added to food in homes across China. It is an effective and very safe qi tonic, and can be used to boost energy and strengthen the lungs and spleen. It can be used as a restorative when there is fatigue or low energy due to illness or over-exertion.

The Dangers of Genetic Engineering for Vegetarians

by Ronald Epstein, Ph.D.

In the early 1990's I read that scientists were putting insect and animal genes in vegetables. As a vegetarian I was very concerned, because I didn't want to eat vegetables that had insect and animal genes in them. I felt that this violated Buddhist principles about pure vegetarian food, and so I started looking into this matter. Not only did I find out that such vegetables were actually being developed, but I also found out that some scientists were putting human genes into vegetables. Since there were no laws to require labeling of GMO vegetables, there was no way to know whether you were eating pure vegetables or vegetables with weird genes in them. In 1993 I wrote a short article for Vajra Bodhi Sea (a Buddhist magazine) about the dangers of genetic engineering for vegetarians, because I wanted all of the members of Dharma Realm Buddhist Association to become aware of the problem. The Master asked me why I wrote the article, and I said, "Well, I think this development in science and technology is very dangerous. It goes against Buddhist principles, and it's going to not be good for the environment." The Master then told me that it was good that I had written the article. If we didn't do something about it, genetic engineering would cause tremendous damage to the world. He then strongly encouraged me to continue to write about the dangers of genetic engineering.

What can we do about the situation? For a start, we can educate ourselves about what is happening. Then we can inform our governments and elected officials and urge them to do whatever is possible to inform the public, label foods, prevent the most blatant dangers, and slow down the progress on the road toward major disaster.

"Buddhism and Measure H," Vajra Bodhi Sea: A Monthly Journal of Orthodox Buddhism, April, 2004, pp. 39–43.

For more information, visit online.sfsu.edu/rone/OnlinePublications.htm

If everyone becomes vegetarian and protects life
Disasters in the world will disappear into thin air.
—Venerable Master Hsuan Hua (1918–1995)

I strolled at leisure by the pond,
To watch the fish afloat,
And met two youths with bait and rod,
In their fishing boat.

With different hearts we take delight
In watching perch and trout,
I have come to feed the fish,
They've come to hook them out.

   —Bai Juyi (Tang Dynasty, 618–906) from Kindness

A Healthy and Simple Solution for a Happy Life

Natural ingredients,

Simple directions,

Effortless cooking,

Relaxed and enjoyable meals;

Delicious yet balanced in nutrition —

Culinary art.

—Dharma Realm Cookbook Team

B. Easy Side Dishes

1. Simmered Cabbage with Shitake Mushrooms and Lily Flowers

Makes 4 to 6 servings

Ingredients

6 dried shitake mushrooms
1 cup lily flowers
1 cabbage, cut into 6 sections
2–3 tablespoons low-salt soy sauce

Directions

- Soak the shitake mushrooms in hot water for fifteen minutes, or until soft. Rinse well to remove the grit and squeeze out the water. Trim the stems and julienne.
- Soak the lily flowers for about ten minutes and drain well. Trim the stems and tie the lily flowers into knots (optional). See picture on opposite page.
- Place the cabbage in a pot with enough water to cover. Bring to a boil.
- Stir in the mushrooms, lily flowers and soy sauce. Return to a boil. Cover and reduce the heat to low. Simmer for thirty minutes.
- Transfer to a warm serving dish and serve immediately.

Tip

Purchase cabbage with a pointed head. It will remain fresh for up to one month in the crisper in the refrigerator.

Information

Lily Flowers: The common day lily. All parts of the day lily—the sprouting leaves that appear in the spring, the summer buds and blossoms, and even the rhizomes—are edible. The buds, known as "golden needles," have a long history in Chinese cuisine and medicine. In the United States, they are considered a delicacy by wild food gatherers.

In Chinese medicine, lily flowers are used to enrich the blood and energy, strengthen tendons and bones and widen the chest cavity. They also treat depression, forgetfulness and insomnia. Sailors who are vegetarian often use them as the primary staple in their diet.

Lily flowers should be completely cooked before being eaten, because they contain a substance called colchicine that may cause an allergic reaction.

Shitake Mushrooms (ala black mushrooms)

An edible fungus native to Asia and grown in forests. They can be found throughout the year in supermarket shelves across the United States.

Chinese medicine considers shitake mushrooms to be cooling in nature with a bitter taste. They reduce tumors, lower cholesterol and prevent thrombosis; eliminate excess mucus from the lungs; strengthen the stomach and increase the appetite. They contain antibiotic properties and help to discharge toxins accumulated from animal products. They also contain protein, vitamin D-1 and vitamin B complex, as well as ten fatty acids of which seven are essential.

2. Avocado Tofu Salad with Sesame-Seaweed Mix

Makes 4 servings

Ingredients

½ block silken tofu, rinsed and cubed

½ avocado, peeled and cubed

½ tablespoon soy sauce paste, diluted in a little water

1 tablespoon sesame-seaweed mix

Directions

- Arrange the tofu and avocado cubes on a serving plate. Top with the soy sauce mixture and sprinkle with the sesame-seaweed mix. Serve cold.

Tip

Sprinkle on the sesame-seaweed mix right before serving so it does not become soggy and lose its flavor and crunchiness. Lemon juice helps avocado to retain its bright color.

Information

Avocado: Chinese medicine considers avocado to have a cooling nature and sweet flavor. It contains fat and protein that are easily digested, harmonizes the liver, lowers cholesterol and prevents heart disease. It is rich in vitamins B, C, E, fiber and copper that aids in blood cell formation. Abundant in anti-oxidants, it beautifies the skin and slows aging. People who crave fats, but cannot tolerate poor fatty foods, do well with avocados. *Guinness World Records* ranks avocado as the highest fruit in nutritional value. It is often recommended for nursing mothers.

We shouldn't use names such as 'vegetarian chicken,' 'vegetarian duck,'
and 'vegetarian abalone' for vegetarian dishes.
If we are vegetarians, why can't we forget about meat?
The mere use of such names plants seeds of impurity.
Vegetarian dishes shouldn't be called by non-vegetarian names.

   —Venerable Master Hsuan Hua (1918–1995)

3. Wild String Beans with Toasted Black Sesame Seed

Makes 4 servings

Ingredients

2 ¼ cups (10 oz/300 g) string beans,
    stringed and cut in half

Black sesame seed, toasted

½ tablespoon salt

Toasted sesame oil

Directions

- Blanch the string beans until more than half-cooked and still bright green.
- Add the salt and drizzle with sesame oil. Toss well and transfer to a warm serving dish.
- Sprinkle with the toasted sesame seed and serve immediately.

Tip

Select string beans that are dark green and firm.

Information

String Beans: Chinese medicine considers string beans to have a neutral thermal nature and sweet flavor. They strengthen the kidneys and produce blood cells; clarify vision; act as a laxative; prevent athlete's foot; and treat diarrhea and the frequent urination and thirst that accompany diabetes.

Caution

String beans contain two poisonous elements — red blood cell agglutinant and saponin — both of which stimulate the gastrointestinal system and coagulate red blood cells. Fortunately, they can be destroyed by a temperature above 100 degree C. For this reason, string beans must be completely cooked.

All creatures feel pain when they're hurt.
Even bugs and ants long to live.
Creatures' lives were given to them by nature,
Tell children not to take life lightly.
    —The Fool of Rong Lake (Qing Dynasty, 1644–1911) from Kindness

4. Crispy Tofu

Makes 4 servings

Ingredients

1 block silken tofu (12–16 oz/340–450 g)
½ tablespoon soy sauce
¼ cup (2 fl oz/59 ml) water
¼ cup dried vegetarian floss (textured soy protein sprinkle)
Celery, shredded

Directions

- Rinse tofu and drain. Cut into ½-inch (1.3 cm) slices. Arrange on a serving dish.
- Combine the soy sauce and water in a saucepan. Bring to a boil. Remove from the heat and pour over the tofu.
- Sprinkle the dried floss and celery on top of the tofu and serve immediately.

Tip

Sprinkle with the dried floss right before serving, so it will not be soggy and lose its flavor.

Information

Tofu: Made from soy milk in much the same way as cheese is made from milk. It contains twice as much protein as milk, but is low in saturated fat and cholesterol free, making it a good protein for the elderly. Rich in calcium, magnesium and iron, it benefits bones; cleanses the blood vessels and heart; restores the pancreas (in diabetes); lowers fevers; protects against atherosclerosis and bone loss; and boosts milk in mothers. Tofu also contains the eight essential amino acids and lecithin, a natural brain food.

Silken Tofu

A low-fat tofu with a smooth, creamy texture--an excellent substitute for eggs and dairy products used in baked goods. It does need to be precooked.

Caution

Commercially prepared soy milk, infant soy formulas, soy protein powders and soy concentrates often contain denatured proteins and cannot be digested well. Generally, they do not promote lasting health, especially in children. Use only organic tofu.

A person of the deepest spirituality will also have a tender concern for every aspect of creation. Such an individual could no more harm a living creature than he or she could harm himself or herself.
    —Ven. Sunyana Graef (1948–   ), *The Foundation of Ecology in Zen Buddhism*

5. Tofu Strings with Red and Green Peppers

Makes 4 to 6 servings

Ingredients

10 ounces (300 g) soft dried tofu strings
1 tablespoon oil
1 cup (8 fl oz/250 ml) water
Green and red peppers, thinly sliced
½ tablespoon salt
2 slices ginger
Toasted sesame oil

Directions

- Blanch the tofu strings.
- In a wok or skillet, heat the oil over medium high. Add the oil. Just before it begins to smoke, add the ginger and stir-fry for one to two minutes, or until aromatic.
- Add the water and bring to a boil. Stir in the tofu strings and season with salt.
- Cook for two minutes. Transfer to a warm serving dish. Drizzle with the sesame oil and garnish with pepper slices. Serve immediately.

Variation

Substitute Japanese cucumbers for the peppers.

Tip

If the dried tofu strings are not the soft type, add salt and vinegar while cooking to soften them.

Information

Tofu Strings: Chinese legend ascribes the invention of tofu to Prince Liu An over two thousand years ago. Famous dishes such as "Snow Cloud Broth," and "Five-Spices Tofu," appeared in the Song Dynasty (960–1279). During the Qing Dynasty 1644–1911, a Yangzhou chef created "Enhanced Tofu Strings." To commemorate this event, layman Xingan of that era wrote a poem called "Gazing at Jiangnan." This is probably the earliest poem about dried tofu strings. Nothing more is known about the author other than his name and the poem on page 83.

Yangzhou is so splendid
Guests are invited to tea.
Enhanced tofu strings,
Piles of thin threads,
Copper pipes stretch out like long shoots,
Warm spirits and crystalline dishes.

6. Konnyaku with Wasabi Mayonnaise (A Japanese dish)

Makes 4 to 6 servings

Ingredients

1 ½ pounds (20 oz/600 g) white konnyaku (yam cake)

2 ½ tablespoon Wasabi mayonnaise sauce (see recipe below)

Directions

- Blanch the konnyaku. Cut into halves and transfer to a serving dish.

  Make Wasabi Mayonnaise Sauce by combining 2 tablespoons eggless mayonnaise and ½ tablespoon wasabi mustard.

- Combine ingredients and spoon over the konnyaku.

- Serve warm or cold.

Variations

Add soy sauce to wasabi mayonnaise sauce for a tastier dish. Or add a mixture of grated ginger, soy sauce paste, white vinegar, and toasted sesame oil.

Tip

Konnyaku can be refrigerated but not frozen; freezing makes it very hard.

One is not a great one because one defeats or harms other living beings. One is so called because one refrains from defeating or harming other living beings.

　—The Buddha (563–483 B.C.) from The Dhammapada, Ch. 19

7. Black and White Cloud Ears with Ginger

Makes 4 to 6 servings

Ingredients

2 ¼ cups (10 oz/300 g) black cloud ears
    (black fungus)

2 cups (9 oz/275 g) white cloud ears
    (white fungus)

1 tablespoon oil

1 cup ginger, julienned

1-2 tablespoons soy sauce

2 cups (1 pint/500 ml) homemade broth or water

Directions

- Soak the cloud ears in warm water for fifteen minutes. Drain well. Trim the hard parts and tear into small pieces by hand.
- Heat a wok or skillet over medium-high heat. Add the oil. Just before it begins to smoke, add the ginger and stir-fry for one to two minutes, or until aromatic. Add the soy sauce and cook for one minute, stirring constantly.
- Add the cloud ears and continue to stir-fry for three to four more minutes. Stir in the broth and simmer until soft, about three minutes.
- Transfer to a warm serving dish and serve immediately.

Variation

Add pineapple slices for a unique flavor.

Tip

Use fresh cloud fungi when possible because they contain more calcium than dried fungi.

Information

Cloud Ears: Edible fungus that can be black or white. It is rich in protein, fat, innate sugar, minerals, carotene, phosphorus, and vitamins. It contains a natural gelatin and polysaccharides that help prevent cancer.

Caution

The black cloud ears contain blood thinner and should be eaten sparingly—in small amounts and not too often.

Being a vegetarian helped me to become an all-around athlete. Vegetarian food supplies me with the energy I need to enjoy a healthy and fulfilling life.

—Sally Eastall, Gold Metal marathon runner (1963–   )

8. Sesame Spinach

Makes 4 to 6 servings

Ingredients

1 ¼ pounds (20 oz/600 g) chopped spinach
2 cups (16 fl oz/473 ml) homemade broth
1 tablespoon soy sauce
½ tablespoon sugar or equivalent sweetener
Sesame seed, toasted

Directions

- Blanch the spinach and transfer to a warm serving dish.
- Bring the broth to a boil. Add the soy sauce and sweetener. Cook for about one minute and remove from the heat.
- Pour the broth over the spinach and sprinkle with toasted sesame seed. Serve immediately.

Variation

Use Chinese broccoli instead of spinach.

Information

Spinach: Chinese medicine considers spinach to be cooling in nature with a sweet flavor. It has the reputation of being "the king of vegetables," with an abundance of protein, iron, sulfur, and chlorophyll that build the blood and cleanse it of toxins; treats nosebleed; moistens dryness and quenches thirst, particular in diabetes. It is rich in vitamin A, treats night blindness, B1, B2 and C. The red part of the spinach root contains vitamin K, which is absent in most fruits and vegetables. It is helpful in preventing bleeding of the skin and internal organs.

Caution

Although spinach is high in calcium and nutrients, it contains phylic acid which contributes to bone loss and kidney stones. Blanching spinach helps to neutralize the phylic acid to some extent. Use spinach sparingly. Avoid eating tofu and spinach together.

*I do not see any reason why animals should be slaughtered
to serve as human diet when there are so many substitutes.
After all, man can live without meat.*

—The Dalai Lama (1935–   )

9. Sweet Konnyaku with Chinese 5-Spice Powder

Makes 4 to 6 servings

Ingredients

2 large pieces konnyaku (yam cake)

Shredded carrot and radish for garnish

2 cups (16 oz/473 ml) homemade broth or water

1 Chinese 5-spice powder bag or 1 teaspoon 5-spice powder tied in a bag.

2 tablespoons soy sauce

1 slice ginger

Toasted sesame oil

Directions

- Rinse the konnyaku and slice. Make a cut in the center and push one side through for a decorative effect. See photo.
- Bring the liquid to boil in a pot. Add the konnyaku, spice bag, soy sauce, ginger and oil. Reduce the heat to low. Cover and cook for fifteen to twenty minutes.
- Turn off the heat and steep for ten minutes to absorb the flavor. Drizzle with the sesame oil.
- Transfer to a warm serving dish and garnish with the grated carrots and radish. Serve immediately.

Information

Konnyaku: A Japanese food made from a plant in the taro family, called konnyaku. It is much like a yam. The root is ground into a powder and combined with a coagulating agent to set into a firm cake. It can be used as a thickening agent or for gelling. Konnyaku is effective in controlling diabetes, cholesterol, and obesity. Due to its cleansing function, it helps to prevent cancer of the large intestine and also constipation. One teaspoon of konnyaku powder is equivalent to ten teaspoons of cornstarch.

*People save whatever creature by refraining
from eating that type of creature.*
　　—Venerable Master Hsuan Hua (1918–1995)

10. Fiddlehead Rolls Stuffed with Black Beans

Fiddleheads are the unfurled fronds of a fern, also known as fernbrake or bracken. Both the commercial and wild varieties are edible and can be found in Asian markets.

Makes 4 to 6 servings

Ingredients

1 ¼ pounds (20 oz/600 mg) fiddleheads, rinsed and trimmed

1 tablespoon oil

⅔ cup (5 oz/140 g) fermented black beans

½ tablespoon ginger, grated

¼ tablespoon salt

½ tablespoon sugar or equivalent sweetener

Directions

- Place the fiddleheads in cold water in a large pot (one cup fiddleheads to twenty cups water). Cover and boil for thirty minutes. Let it soak in the water for about six to eight hours or overnight. Drain well and discard the soak water.
- Cut into 2-inch (5 cm) pieces.
- Heat a wok or skillet over medium-high heat. Add the oil. Just before it begins to smoke, add the ginger and stir-fry for one to two minutes, or until aromatic.
- Add the beans, fiddleheads, salt, sugar and pepper. Stir-fry briefly, about two to three minutes. Transfer to a warm serving dish and serve immediately.

Variation

For a crispier and more appetizing dish, stir in ground peanuts before removing from the wok.

Information

Fiddleheads: Refers to common bracken fiddleheads, the immature, tightly curled emerging fronds of ferns. They have been considered edible by many cultures throughout history and are still commonly used today as a foodstuff. Bracken fiddleheads are either consumed fresh, cooked, or preserved by salting, pickling, or sun drying.

Chinese medicine considers fiddleheads to have a cooling nature and sweet flavor. They are diuretic and calming, so they can eliminate heat and neutralize toxins in the body. They contain an abundance of protein, fats, saccharides, fiber, calcium, phosphorus, iron, vitamin A, and vitamin B-complex

Caution

The British Royal Horticultural Society warns against consumption of bracken fiddleheads either by humans or livestock, since it contains carcinogens linked with esophageal and stomach cancer. However, correctly cooked, the carcinogens can be rendered harmless.

What Is the Difference between Killing Vegetables for Food and Killing Animals for Food?

Question:

"When you eat one bowl of rice, you take the life of all the grains of rice, whereas eating meat you take only one animal's life. Where is the compassion in this?"

Venerable Master Hsuan Hua:

"Although the life force of a large number of plants may appear sizeable, it is not as great as that of a single animal or a single mouthful of meat. Take, for example, rice: tens of billions of grains of rice do not contain as much life force as a single piece of meat. At death, the nature changes, the soul scatters, and the smallest fragments become plants. So there is a difference between eating plants and eating animals. What is more, plants have very short life spans. Grass, for example, is born in the spring and dies within months. Animals live a long time. If you don't kill them, they will live for many years. Rice, regardless of conditions, will only live a short time. If you really look into it, there are many factors to consider, and even science hasn't got it all straight."

Question-and-Answer Session with Venerable Master Hua at the City of Ten Thousand Buddhas.

Family-style dishes,
Foremost in health and nutrition.
Elders, mothers-to-be, little ones,
Youths and those in their prime,
Chewing slowly, savoring the flavor.
Happiness for everyone.

—Dharma Realm Cookbook Team

Being a vegetarian makes it easier for us to
increase our loving kindness and compassion.
—Zen Master Thích Nhất Hạnh (1926–   )

C. Main Dishes and Family Fare

1. Luffa with Bamboo Fungus and Red Goji Berries

Makes 4 servings

Ingredients

1 cup bamboo fungus

1 tablespoon oil for sautéing

1 tablespoon fresh ginger, grated

1 luffa, peeled and cut into chunks

½ tablespoon salt

1 tablespoon red goji berries (see page 119)

Directions

- Soak the bamboo fungus for twenty minutes in warm water. Drain and cut into bite-size pieces.
- In a skillet, heat the oil on medium heat. Sauté the ginger for one to two minutes, or until aromatic. Add the luffa and stir lightly. Next add the bamboo fungus.
- Reduce the heat to medium. Cook for three minutes. Add the salt and stir well to mix.
- Transfer to a warm serving dish. Sprinkle the goji berries on top and serve immediately.

Tip

Luffa produces its own water during cooking, so it is not necessary to add liquid.

Variation

Add basil at the end of cooking for a different taste.

Information

Bamboo Fungus: A fungus that grows among bamboo forests in Asia. It also grows in woodlands and gardens in Africa, the Americas, and Australia. It is characterized by a bell-shaped cap and a delicate lacy skirt. With its beauty and delightful flavor, it has been regarded throughout Chinese history as a delicacy.

Bamboo fungus contains high protein, fat and eight kinds of amino acids that the human body needs. It aids the eyes and lungs, reduces blood pressure and cholesterol, and prevents cancer. It strengthens the body, delays old age, and is a natural antiseptic.

A genus of the cucumber family and similar to a gourd. When harvested at a young stage, it is a popular vegetable in China and Vietnam. When dry, it can be used as a scrubbing sponge or boiled in water for medicine. Luffa is used to treat colds, swelling and sinus problems, arthritis pain, muscle pain, and chest pain, and to detoxify the skin. Nursing mothers use it to increase milk flow.

Around this lonely mountain top myriad peaks revolve,
I've come to cultivate an ascetic's disciplined resolve.
I take my broom and sweep away the deer tracks in the snow;
The deer passed by, but in the morning, hunters will not know.
—Lu Fuhuang, Tang Dynasty (618–906), *Kindness*

2. Wishing-You-Well Soybean Sprouts with Licorice-Flavored Water

Makes 4 to 6 servings

Ingredients

10 ounces (300 g) Shanghai bok choy

1 tablespoon oil for stir-fry

10 ounces (300 g) soybean sprouts

1 cup (8 fl oz/250 ml) homemade broth
  or water

¼ carrot, sliced diagonally

½ tablespoon salt

Licorice-Flavored Water

½ slice or 1 tablespoon shredded licorice

2 tablespoons water

Directions

- Blanch the bok choy and set aside.
- Soak the licorice in the water and set aside.
- Heat a wok or skillet over medium-high heat. Add the oil. Just before it begins to smoke, add the ginger and stir-fry for one to two minutes, or until aromatic.
- Add the soybean sprouts. Stir-fry for two minutes. Add the broth and bring to a boil. Reduce the heat to low and simmer for five minutes.
- Drain the licorice and discard. Add the licorice water to the wok along with the bok choy, carrots and salt. Stir-fry for one to two minutes until the vegetables are almost done, but still bright in color.
- Transfer to a warm serving dish and serve immediately.

Information

Soybean Sprouts: Shaped like a Chinese jade ornament called *ruyi*, which means "wishing you well." Used primarily in Chinese cuisine, soybean sprouts contain raw protein, amino acids, and minerals such as calcium, phosphorus, iron, zinc and vitamins. They are especially high in vitamin C. Research indicates that soybean sprouts protect against atherosclerosis and bone loss.

Chinese Licorice Root (gan cao)

Has a sweet taste and is about five hundred times sweeter than cane sugar. In Chinese medicine, it is used to treat spleen and stomach weakness, tiredness and lack of strength, palpitations and shortness of breath and coughs with abundance of phlegm. It is anti-inflammatory, anti-oxidant, antiviral, anti-allergic, anti-cancer, and an important ingredient in cough drops and syrups.

Caution

Licorice is considered safe in moderate doses, although it may increase blood pressure and heart rate in very large doses. Be cautious if you have hypertension or heart disease.

3. Braised Peanuts with Seaweed and Gluten Balls

Makes 4 to 6 servings

Ingredients

1 ½ cups (10 oz/300 g) peanuts, shelled

12 inches (30 cm) kombu seaweed
  (see page 10)

1 cup (4 oz/120 g) fried gluten balls,
  blanched

6 cups (1 ½ quarts/liters) hot homemade broth or water

1 tablespoon soy sauce

Directions

- Add two parts water to one part peanuts in a pot. Bring to a boil. Reduce the heat to low. Cover and simmer until the peanuts are soft, about one hour. Drain well.

- Do not wipe the kombu prior to use as the white powder adds flavor. Remove dirt if you see any. Then soak the kombu in cold water for twenty minutes, until tender enough to cut. Drain well. Cut into 2-inch (5 cm) wide pieces.

- Add kombu, gluten and soy sauce to the peanuts. Bring to a boil and reduce the heat to low. Cover and simmer until seaweed is soft, about twenty to thirty minutes.

- Transfer to a warm serving dish and serve immediately.

Tip

Use shelled peanuts that are full-bodied and light in color for stir-frying or stewing. Discard the ones that are discolored. The best quality peanuts are those that are in season.

Information

Storing Seaweed: Seaweed can be kept in the refrigerator for a long time in an airtight container with a desiccating agent. Some commonly used desiccants are silica gel, activated charcoal and calcium sulfate. If seaweed becomes brown and moldy, do not eat it.

The Buddha's teaching leads us to the realization that we must always strive to harm no sentient being, human or nonhuman, whether or not it is in our selfish interest to do so.

—Norm Phelps, *The Great Compassion: Buddhism & Animal Rights*

4. Cabbage with Corn, Edamame, and Button Mushrooms

Makes 4 to 6 servings

Ingredients

1 cabbage

2 cups (16 fl oz/475 ml) homemade broth
    or water

1 potato, peeled and cubed

¼ carrot, cubed

1 tablespoon edamame

2 cups white button mushrooms,
    thinly sliced

¾ cup (5 oz/140 g) corn kernels

½ tablespoon salt

Toasted sesame oil

Thick Sauce

1 tablespoon oil for sauté

2 tablespoons brown rice flour

3 tablespoons water

Tip

Cook cabbage in tune with the seasons. In the summer, cook it for a short time with little or no water over high heat to retain vitamins and freshness. In the winter, cook it for a longer time on low heat to break down the cellulose structure, making the minerals and other nutrients more accessible. This also gives the cabbage a sweeter taste and makes it more warming.

Directions

- Make the thick sauce: Pan-roast or sauté the flour in oil for one to two minutes. Add two to three tablespoons of water to make a thick sauce, stirring constantly. Remove from heat and set aside.

- Remove the cabbage core (save to make broth later). Blanch the entire cabbage until fully cooked. Transfer to a warm serving dish. Set aside.

- Leave two cups of the water in the same pot and bring to a boil. Add the potato, carrot and edamame. Reduce the heat to medium and boil for five minutes.

- Add the mushrooms, corn and salt. Return to a boil.

- Stir in the prepared thick sauce and mix well. Reduce heat to low and simmer for five minutes, stirring frequently. Add a few drops of the sesame oil at end of cooking.

- Pour the entire mixture over the cabbage. Serve immediately.

Caution

Corn may be genetically modified, so it is best to use organic. Commercial creamed corn usually contains dairy.

Information

Edamame: Immature soybeans in the pod, found in the cuisine of Japan, China and Hawaii. Salt-boiled edamame in pods are eaten by squeezing beans out of pods with fingers. They are a great appetizer!

Most of the health benefits of edamame are a result of its high protein content. It is also rich in minerals such as phosphorus, calcium, sodium, iron and vitamins A and C.

In Chinese traditional medicine, edamame is useful for appropriate functioning of the stomach, kidney, heart, liver and the excretory system. The oil from soybean is considered healthy because of its high concentrations of unsaturated fatty acids.

5. Burdock with Carrot and Toasted Sesame Seed

Makes 4 to 6 servings

Ingredients

1 burdock root, julienned

½ tablespoon oil for sauté

½ part water to 1 part burdock root

¼ carrot, julienned

2 tablespoons low-salt soy sauce

½ tablespoon sugar or
   equivalent sweetener

1 tablespoon toasted sesame seed

Directions

- In a skillet, heat the oil and sauté the burdock for one to two minutes. Add the water and reduce the heat to low. Cover and simmer for six minutes.
- Stir in the sweetener and carrot. Simmer two minutes.
- Transfer to a warm serving dish. Sprinkle toasted sesame seeds on top and serve immediately.

Tip

To keep burdock root from turning brown, place in a bowl of cold water with two tablespoons white vinegar or lemon juice. Purchase roots that are smooth and heavy, and flex when waved in the air.

Information

Burdock Root: The taproot of the young burdock plant. It is very crisp and has a sweet, mild and pungent flavor with a little muddy harshness that can be reduced by soaking shredded roots in water for five to ten minutes.

Burdock root contains a large amount of roughage, protein, vitamins and minerals such as potassium, iron, calcium and phosphate. The roughage induces intestinal movements, relieves constipation, reduces inflammation and produces sweating to excrete toxins that are lodged in tendons and joints.

The key to longevity is to get up early, live purely, and control one's diet. If one follows this, one will definitely be free of desire and anger, passing the day in leisure. This is how longevity is acquired.

—Elder Master Empty Cloud (1840–1959)

6. Tofu with Tomatoes and Lima Beans

Makes 4 to 6 servings

Ingredients

1 cup fresh, canned, or frozen lima beans

½ tablespoon oil for stir-fry

2 tomatoes, cubed

1 block tofu, rinsed and cubed
(12–14 oz/340–450 g)

1 tablespoon salt

1 tablespoon sugar or equivalent sweetener

1 cup (8 fl oz/250 ml) homemade broth or water

Thickener

2 tablespoons arrowroot powder

2 tablespoons cold water

Tip

If using dried lima beans, soak them in water overnight for faster cooking, better digestibility and gas prevention. Drain thoroughly and add fresh water before cooking.

Directions

- Blanch the lima beans
- Heat a wok or skillet over medium-high heat. Add the oil. Just before it begins to smoke, add the tomatoes and stir-fry for two minutes.
- Add the tofu, lima beans, salt and sweetener. Stir-fry for two minutes. Add the broth and reduce heat to low. Cover and simmer for five minutes, stirring frequently.
- Mix the arrowroot powder and water together. Slowly add the mixture to the wok to make a thin sauce. Simmer about three minutes, stirring frequently.
- Transfer to a warm serving dish and serve immediately.

Variation

Make this into a simple dish without lima beans.

Information

Lima Beans: Chinese medicine considers lima beans to have a cool nature and sweet flavor. They benefit the liver and lungs, neutralize acidic conditions that exist due to consumption of refined food and meat, and are highly alkalizing. Among legumes, they contain the highest amounts of carotene, protein, vitamins and minerals and are highest in iron, calcium, zinc, phosphate and potassium

Caution

Those who become bloated after meals should only consume lima beans in small amounts.

*Eating vegetarian food will reduce desire, bringing about
contentment and positive thinking. Your energy and blood
will be clear rather than murky.*
    —Venerable Master Hsuan Hua (1918–1995)

7. Sweet and Sour Konnyaku with Asparagus, Miniature Corn, and Plum Tomatoes

Makes 4 to 6 servings

Ingredients

2 cups miniature corn

10 ounces (300 mg) asparagus, cut into
    1½-inch (5 cm) lengths

2 cups (16 fl oz/500 ml) konnyaku,
    (see page 36)

A few plum tomatoes

Sweet and Sour Sauce

½ tablespoon ginger, grated

½ tablespoon white vinegar

¾ teaspoon sugar or equivalent sweetener

1 tablespoon soy sauce paste

Toasted sesame oil

Directions

- Combine the ingredients to make the Sweet and Sour Sauce. Set aside.
- Blanch the miniature corn, asparagus and konnyaku, separately.
- Transfer to a serving platter and garnish with plum tomatoes. Pour the sauce over the vegetables or serve as a dipping sauce.

Variation

Use cubed konnyaku for a different effect.

Information

Asparagus: There are two kinds — green and white. The nutritional value of the green asparagus is the higher of the two, especially in vitamins and iron. Chinese medicine considers asparagus to be warm in nature and slightly bitter and pungent. It contains the diuretic asparagine that helps to eliminate urine from the kidneys. It also treats kidney infections, heart disease, hepatitis, cirrhosis, edema, diabetes, hypertension, lung congestion and coughing; increases the appetite and suppresses cancer cells.

Having a merciful and compassionate heart will show up in all aspects of one's life, but the simplest and most direct way is to follow a vegetarian diet.

—Lin Ching Shywan, *A Buddhist Perspective on Vegetarianism*

8. Spring Snow

Makes 4 to 6 servings

Ingredients

1 cup edamame (see page 110)

1 tablespoon oil for stir fry

3 tofu pouches, rinsed and cut into ½-inch (2 cm) long strips

1 tablespoon low-salt soy sauce

1 hot pepper, diced

2¼ cups (10 oz/300 g) pickled green mustard, rinsed and cut into ½-inch (2 cm) pieces

¾ teaspoon salt

¾ teaspoon sugar or equivalent sweetener

2 tablespoons hot water

Directions

- Blanch the edamame.
- Heat a wok or skillet over medium-high heat. Add the oil. Just before it begins to smoke, add the tofu pouches and stir-fry for two minutes.
- Remove from the wok and set aside. Reheat the wok and add soy sauce, hot peppers and pickled mustard. Stir-fry for a further three minutes.
- Add the edamame, salt, sweetener and water. Reduce heat to low. Simmer for three minutes.
- Transfer to a warm serving dish and serve immediately.

Tip

The best way to retain the green color of green leafy vegetables during cooking is to rinse vegetables with cold water immediately after blanching. Adding baking soda is not a good method because it destroys some vitamin content. Salt does not destroy vitamins but does add sodium chloride.

I know, in my soul, that to eat a creature who is raised to be eaten,
and who never has a chance to be a real being, is unhealthy.
It's like . . . you're just eating misery. You're eating a bitter life.
   —Alice Walker, Pulitzer Prize-winning novelist (1944–   )

9. Braised Bamboo Shoots with Shitake Mushrooms

Makes 4 to 6 servings

Ingredients

5 dried shitake mushrooms

10 ounces (300 g) bamboo shoots, peeled and cut into ¾-inch (2.5 cm) diagonal pieces

3 gluten rolls, cut into ¾-inch (2.5 cm) cubes

2 cups (16 fl oz/475 ml) homemade broth or water

1 tablespoon soy sauce

½ tablespoon sugar or equivalent sweetener

¾ teaspoon salt

3 slices ginger

Toasted sesame oil

Tip

It is not necessary to deep-fry the gluten. If cooked directly, it is still tasty, saves time, and is easier to digest.

Directions

- Soak the mushrooms in warm water for about twenty minutes, or until soft. Rinse well to remove the grit and squeeze out the water. Trim the stems and julienne.
- Fry the gluten in batches for one to two minutes, until golden brown. Drain on absorbent towels.
- Bring the broth to a boil in a saucepan. Add the mushrooms, bamboo shoots, soy sauce, sweetener, salt and ginger. Return to a boil. Reduce to low heat.
- Add the fried gluten and simmer about eight minutes. Sprinkle with sesame oil at the end of cooking.
- Transfer to a warm serving dish and serve immediately.

One should treat animals such as deer, camels, asses, monkeys, mice, snakes, birds and flies exactly like one's own son. How little difference there actually is between children and these innocent animals.
—Srimad Bhagavatam, 7.14.9, an ancient Vedic text

10. Ginkgo Nuts with Cloud Ears and Lily Flowers

Makes 4 to 6 servings

Ingredients

1 cup lily flowers (see page 74)

1 cup cloud ears (see page 86)

1 cup fresh ginkgo nuts

1 tablespoon oil for sauté

2 cups (16 fl oz/475 ml) homemade
    broth or water

¾ teaspoon salt

½ tablespoon sugar or equivalent sweetener

½ tablespoon low-salt soy sauce

Directions

- Soak the lily flowers for about ten minutes and drain well. Trim the stems.
- Soak the cloud ears in warm water about twenty minutes and drain well. Tear the cloud ears into ¾-inch pieces by hand.
- Blanch the ginkgo nuts.
- In a skillet, heat the oil and sauté the cloud ears for two minutes. Add the sweetener, soy sauce and broth. Cover and bring to a boil. Reduce heat and simmer for three minutes.
- Add the remaining ingredients and cook for two more minutes.
- Transfer to a warm serving dish and serve immediately.

Information

Ginkgo Nuts: The seeds of the ginkgo tree (Ginkgo biloba). *Botanical.com* describes them as "the oldest living trees on the earth, some over 3,000 years old . . . were nearly wiped out during the Ice Age everywhere except in China." It is found in monasteries in the mountains and in temple gardens, where, since about 1100 A.D., Buddhist monks have cultivated the tree for its many good qualities.

Caution

Ginkgo nuts are potentially toxic when uncooked and should be eaten sparingly, no more than five to ten in a day.

Vegetables, fruit, and grain should compose our diet. Not an ounce of meat should enter our stomachs. The eating of meat is unnatural. We are to return to God's original purpose in the creation of man.
—Ellen White, co-founder of the Seventh Day Adventist Church (1827–1915)

11. Sweet and Sour Golden Nuggets

Makes 4 to 6 servings

Ingredients

2 cups textured vegetarian protein chunks*

1 tablespoon soy sauce

Oil for frying

1 carrot, cut into chunks

2 potatoes, peeled and cut into chunks

2 cups (16 fl oz/475 ml) homemade broth
    or water

1 green bell pepper, cut into chunks

Sweet and Sour Tomato Sauce

3 tablespoons tomato paste

½ tablespoon rice vinegar

½ teaspoon salt

½ teaspoon sugar or equivalent sweetener

Tip

The greener and brighter the green peppers, the fresher they are. Avoid buying old ones with wrinkled skin.

Directions

- Marinate the textured vegetarian protein chunks in the soy sauce for thirty minutes. Then fry them in batches, for one to two minutes, until golden. Drain on absorbent towels. Set aside.

- Bring the broth to a boil in a pot. Add the carrots and potatoes and cook for ten minutes, until almost tender. Add the pepper and textured vegetarian protein chunks. Continue to cook for five minutes until the pepper becomes bright green.

- Make the sweet and sour sauce by combining the tomato paste, rice vinegar, salt and sweetener. Stir the sauce into the pot with the textured vegetarian protein chunks and cook about two to three minutes.

- Transfer to a warm serving dish and serve immediately.

*You can buy marinated textured vegetarian protein chunks, instead of making them.

Information

Green peppers: Originally from South America. They are rich in vitamin C and also vitamin P, which prevents the oxidation of vitamin C. Frequent ingestion of green peppers alleviates fatigue, prevents cancer, promotes smooth skin, erases freckles, improves the appetite, reduces swellings, treats cancer and is anti-aging.

Man did not weave the web of life: he is merely a strand
in it. Whatever he does to the web, he does to himself.
To harm the earth is to heap contempt on its creator.
— Native American Chief (1854)

12. Goji Berry Tofu Pouches with Shitake Mushrooms and Green Peas

Makes 4 to 6 servings

Ingredients

2 dried shitake mushrooms

3 slices thick tofu pouch

1 cup goji berries

1 tablespoon oil for frying

1 tablespoon goji berries

1 tablespoon green peas

2 tablespoons ginger, grated

2–3 tablespoons low-salt soy sauce

1 tablespoon sugar or equivalent sweetener

1½ cups (12 fl oz/350 ml) water

Thickener

2 tablespoons arrowroot powder

2 tablespoons cold water

Directions

- Soak the mushrooms in warm water for about twenty minutes, or until soft. Rinse well to remove the grit and squeeze out the water. Trim the stems and slice thinly.

- Blanch the green peas and set aside.

- Fry the tofu pouches in batches for one to two minutes, until golden. Drain on absorbent towels. Set aside.

- Heat a wok or skillet over medium-high heat. Add the oil. Just before it begins to smoke, add the ginger and stir about one to two minutes, or until aromatic.

- Add the mushrooms and stir-fry for two minutes. Stir in the soy sauce, sweetener, and water. Bring to a boil. Add the tofu pouches and the cup of goji berries.

- Cook for another two to three minutes, stirring to mix well.

- Mix the arrowroot powder and water. Slowly add to the wok to make a thin sauce.

- Simmer about three minutes, stirring occasionally.

- Transfer to a warm serving dish. Sprinkle the green peas and tablespoon of goji berries on top. Serve immediately.

Substitute strips of gluten for the tofu pouches.

Goji berries: Recognized for their health benefits for centuries amongst Tibetan and Himalayan monks. They contain antioxidants that are essential for reducing the number of free radicals within the body; an excess of free radicals causes cell damage and leads to fatigue. High in vitamin C, goji berries treat diabetes, high blood pressure, fever, and age-related eye problems. Some studies using goji berry juice found benefits in mental well-being and calmness, athletic performance, happiness, quality of sleep, and feelings of good health. Goji berries are eaten raw, cooked, or dried and are used in herbal teas, juices, wines and medicines.

13. Bitter Melon with Preserved Turnip Tops

Makes 4 to 6 servings

Ingredients

1 white bitter melon, cut into sections
1½ × 2 inches (4 × 5 cm)

2 cups preserved sweet and salty turnip
tops, rinsed and thinly sliced

2 cups (16 fl oz/500 ml) homemade
broth or water

½ tablespoon soy sauce

1 tablespoon sesame oil

Directions

- Blanch the bitter melon to remove some of its bitterness.
- Place the melon and salted turnip in the inner pot of a rice cooker. Add the broth, soy sauce and oil. Mix well.
- Pour one cup of water in the outer pot of the rice cooker. Steam for about fifteen minutes, or until almost cooked. Leave covered for ten minutes until completely cooked. The rice cooker will automatically turn off when all the water has evaporated.
- Transfer to a warm serving dish and serve immediately.

Variation

Replace salted turnip with fermented black beans.

Information

Bitter Melons: Originated in India and were carried to China in the 14th century. The young shoots and leaves may also be eaten. The melon may taste bitter, but it can sweeten your health. It is one of the most powerful natural antioxidants and an excellent source of flavonoids and vitamin A, all of which play a role in preventing aging, cancers and various diseases. In Chinese medicine, bitter melon eliminates heat symptoms, relieves fatigue, purifies the heart, increases acuity, and enriches the skin. It is also thought to lower blood sugar levels and treat type-2 diabetes.

Tip

Instead of a rice cooker, you can use a double boiler or braise in a saucepan.

The term 'vegan' refers to one that does not eat animals, but also any animal products or derivatives, including milk, cheese, honey; or using animal furs, leathers, skins, etc. The Buddha recommended that pure Bodhisattvas follow this ideal.
— Michael Ohlsson, "The Buddhist Diet"

14. Tofu with Shredded Carrot and Thin Sauce

Makes 4 to 6 servings

Ingredients

1 tablespoon carrot, finely shredded

1 block silken tofu(12–16 oz/340–450 g), rinsed and cubed

1 tablespoon oil for stir-fry

½ tablespoon salt

1 cup (8 fl oz/250 ml) homemade broth or water

½ tablespoon green peas, cooked

Toasted sesame oil

Thin Sauce

2 tablespoons arrowroot powder

1 tablespoon cold water

Tip

Silken tofu can be easily broken into pieces by shaking the pan while cooking.

Directions

- Heat a wok or a skillet over medium-high heat. Add the oil. Just before it begins to smoke, add the carrot puree and stir-fry for one to two minutes.
- Stir in the broth and bring to a boil. Add the tofu and salt. Reduce the heat to low. Simmer for two minutes.
- Mix the arrowroot powder and water together. Slowly add to the wok to make a thin sauce. Simmer about three minutes, stirring occasionally.
- Pour the sauce over the tofu mixture and toss in the green peas. Transfer to a warm serving dish. Drizzle with sesame oil and serve immediately.

Information

Green Peas: There are two types — round peas eaten out of the pods and snow peas eaten pod and all — that are commonly used in Chinese cuisine. Both kinds are rich in vitamins A and C, protein, calcium, iron, phosphorus and some fat. The protein in green peas is easier to digest than that in soy beans. Chinese medicine considers peas to be neutral in nature with a sweet flavor. They are diuretic and tonify the stomach and spleen-pancreas. They also cleanse the blood and treat edema, constipation, boils and morning sickness in pregnant women.

Buddhism regards all living creatures as being endowed with the Buddha nature and the potential to become Buddhas. That's why Buddhism teaches us to refrain from taking the lives of creatures and to protect them instead.
    —Venerable Master Hsuan Hua (1918–1995)

15. Braised Tofu Knots with Shitake Mushrooms

Tofu knots are strips of dried tofu tied into knots.

Makes 4 to 6 servings

Ingredients

3 dried shitake mushrooms

10 ounces (300 g) tofu knots

¼ teaspoon baking soda

1 carrot, cut into wedges

2–3 tablespoons low-salt soy sauce

1 tablespoon sesame oil

½ tablespoon salt

6 cups (1 ½ quarts/liters) water

Directions

- Soak the mushrooms in hot water for twenty minutes, or until soft. Rinse well to remove the grit and squeeze out water. Trim the stems and cut the mushrooms into quarters.
- Blanch the tofu knots with the baking soda.
- Place the tofu knots, mushrooms and carrot in the inner pot of a rice cooker. Stir in the soy sauce, oil, salt and two cups of the water. Add the other two cups of water to the outer pot of the rice cooker. Cook until done, about ten minutes.

Tip

Yellow and orange vegetables such as carrots, pumpkins and tomatoes are minimally affected by cooking. However, to retain the brightness of red vegetables like amaranth and white vegetables like cabbage, daikon radishes, and potatoes, add a bit of vinegar while cooking.

Variation

Braise the ingredients over medium heat in a skillet.

The farmer hoes in the midday sun;
His sweat falls on the soil.
Who can guess how much toil it took
To bring the food to the bowl?
        —Ancient Chinese poem

16. Shanghai Bok Choy with Enoki Mushrooms and Ginger

Makes 4 to 6 servings

Ingredients

3 dried shitake mushrooms

1 bunch enoki mushrooms, trimmed

1 ½ pounds (600 g) Shanghai bok choy

1 tablespoon oil

1 tablespoon ginger, julienned

Carrot for color, julienned

½ tablespoon salt

Toasted sesame oil

Directions

- Soak mushrooms in hot water for twenty minutes, or until soft. Rinse well to remove the grit and squeeze out the water. Trim the stems and julienne.
- Rinse and cut the enoki mushrooms into halves.
- Blanch the bok choy and drain well.
- Heat a wok or skillet over medium-high heat. Add the oil. Just before it begins to smoke, add the ginger and stir-fry for one to two minutes, or until aromatic.
- Add the mushrooms and stir-fry for one to two minutes.
- Add the carrot and stir-fry for more two minutes.
- Add the salt and enoki mushroom.
- Add bok choy and toss to mix well.
- Transfer to a warm serving dish. Drizzle the sesame oil on top and serve immediately.

Tip

Blanch the bok choy and rinse in cold water prior to cooking to retain its fresh taste and bright green color.

Variation

Use Shanghai bok choy in stir-fried vegetable dishes, stews and fried rice.

Information

Enoki Mushrooms: Mushrooms found naturally growing on the stumps of the enoki tree. Medical research conducted in Japan and China finds enoki to have anti-cancer, anti-tumor and anti-viral qualities, and to stimulate the immune system.

Shanghai Bok Choy: A member of the cabbage family. It is cool in nature, sweet and pungent; rich in vitamin C, beta-carotene, fiber and calcium; clears heat; lubricates the intestines; removes stagnant food; quenches thirst and promotes digestion. It contains twice the amount of calcium as milk, and is more easily ingested.

When about 16 years of age, I happen'd to meet with a book, written by one Tryon, recommending a vegetable diet. I determined to go into it. My refusing to eat flesh occasioned an Inconveniency, and I was frequently chided for my singularity.

—Benjamin Franklin (1706–1790), The Autobiography of Benjamin Franklin

17. Stir-Fried Cabbage with Assorted Vegetables

Makes 4 to 6 servings

Ingredients

2 dried shitake mushrooms

1 cloud ear (see page)

1 tablespoon oil

½ cabbage, chopped

¼ carrot, julienned

½ stalk celery, julienned

1 tomato, sliced

2 cups (16 fl oz/500 ml) homemade broth or water

½ tablespoon salt

Directions

- Soak the mushrooms and cloud ear, separately, in hot water for twenty minutes, or until soft. Rinse well to remove the grit and squeeze out the water. Trim the cloud ear and remove the mushroom stems, and then julienne.
- Heat a wok or skillet over medium-high heat. Add the oil. Just before it begins to smoke, add the mushrooms and stir-fry for two minutes.
- Add the cloud ear, cabbage, carrot, celery, tomato and broth. Cook for three minutes, stirring frequently. Add salt and mix well.
- Transfer to a warm serving dish and serve immediately.

If slaughterhouses had glass walls, everyone would be a vegetarian.
    —Paul McCartney, English musician (1942–   )

18. Rice Balls of Three Colors

Makes 3 large rice balls, 6 medium, or 9 small ones

Ingredients

1 cup white rice, cooked

1 cup brown rice, cooked

1 cup red or black rice, cooked

Filling

½ tablespoon nori seaweed paste*

2 tablespoons sesame seaweed mix**

Directions

- Lay a 10"×10" sheet of plastic on a flat surface. Spread one-half of the white rice on top of the sheet.
- Add one third seaweed paste and top with one third sesame seaweed mix. Spread the remaining half cup of white rice on top and even it out.
- Squeeze the ingredients tightly together to form a ball, and then unwrap the rice ball.
- Repeat the steps above using the brown and red or black rice to make two more balls.
- Arrange the three colors of rice balls on a serving dish. Serve cold.

NOTE: Adjust the ingredients to make six medium balls or nine small balls.

---

*Nori seaweed paste is a sweet and salty paste made from nori.

**Sesame seaweed mix is a Japanese condiment. Many store-bought varieties include fish and MSG, so vegetarians should make their own. You can control the amount of salt and sugar, as well as conserve money and packaging. See recipe below:

Sesame Seaweed Mix

Ingredients

2 sheets nori

¼ cup toasted white or black sesame seeds

½ teaspoon coarse sea salt

½ teaspoon sugar or equivalent sweetener

Tip

Rice balls are easier to make with warm rice.

Directions

- Toast the nori over a low flame or burner, waving each sheet over the burner until it is crisp and changes color. Using scissors, cut into small pieces.
- Grind half of the sesame seeds with a mortar and pestle or coffee grinder. Mix with the salt, sweetener, and pieces of nori.
- Add the remaining whole sesame seeds.
- Store in an airtight container.

Information

Nori: Known in the U.S. as a wrap for sushi. It is a red seaweed that grows off the coast of Japan. It has a long history of use in traditional chinese medicine, and is very high in mineral content, especially iodine. A small portion of nori provides well over the adult recommended daily intake of iodine, which is vital for proper thyroid functioning. Nori is also rich in carotenes, vitamin C and vitamin B12, and a beauty aid to skin, hair and nails. It is also called laver.

Saving the Life of a Bee

John was walking down a road with a friend after a rain storm. Stepping over a puddle, he noticed a bee that appeared to have drowned. "I hope you're still alive," he said. Scooping it up gently with his finger, he placed it on dry ground. To his surprise, the bee shook itself and flew away.

Before he knew it a swarm of bees had buzzed around him and landed all over his body. Feeling no fear at all, he stood perfectly still. Streams of energy flowed from the bees into his body, and he felt a peace and happiness that he had never known. The bees flew away as suddenly as they had come, leaving no trace behind.

John and his friend hurried to Master Hua and related what had happened. The Master told them, "This was the bees' way of thanking John for saving one of their kin. You see, life is as precious to them as ours is to us."

Soup is the essence of flavors;
A blending of nutrients a must.
Sip a bowl of soup everyday
For a body healthy and robust.
　　　—Dharma Realm Cookbook Team

D. Heartwarming Soups

I feel very deeply about vegetarianism and the animal kingdom. It was my dog Boycott who led me to question the right of humans to eat other sentient beings.
　　—Cesar Chavez, Co-founder of United Farm Workers (1927–1993)

1. Gold and Silver Refreshing Soup

Makes 4 to 6 servings

Ingredients

1 cup lily flowers (see page 74)

1 white bitter melon (see page 120)

10 cups (2½ quarts/liters) homemade broth or water

2 ears of corn, shucked and cut into 3–4 inch pieces

½ tablespoon salt

Directions

- Soak the lily flowers for ten minutes and drain well. Trim the stems. Set aside
- Cut the bitter melon open and remove the seed. Cut into bite-sized pieces. Set aside.
- Bring the liquid to a boil in a medium-sized pot. Add the corn and bitter melon. Reduce heat to low. Simmer for thirty minutes.
- Add the lily flowers and salt. Cook for two more minutes.
- Transfer to a warm soup bowl and serve hot.

If one spares the lives of other beings, so they can enjoy good health and longevity, then one will receive the same effect too.
    —Venerable Master Hsuan Hua (1918–1995)

2. Celery Tomato Soup

Makes 4 servings

Ingredients

8 cups (2 quarts/liters) homemade broth or water

2 tomatoes, sliced thinly

Salt to taste

1 tablespoon celery, julienned

Directions

- Bring the liquid to boil in a medium-sized pot. Add the tomatoes and bring back to a boil. Reduce the heat to low.
- Add the salt and simmer for five minutes. Stir in the celery.
- Transfer to a warm soup bowl and serve hot.

Information

Celery: Chinese medicine considers celery to have a bitter but pleasant taste and cooling in nature. It clarifies the liver, tonifies the stomach and lowers the blood pressure. If eaten often, celery is beneficial for hypertension, hardening of the arteries, and weak mental status. Celery is rich in phosphorus and calcium, and contains aromatic oil that increases the appetite. Its long crispy stalk makes it one of the most versatile vegetables.

*It's nice to eat a meal and not worry about
what your food may have died of.*

—Dr. J.H. Kellogg (1852–1943), Inventor of corn flakes

3. Dragon Eyes with Fennel

Makes 4 servings

Ingredients

6 cups (1½ quarts/liters) water
1 cup dry longan (dragon eyes)
½ tablespoon black sesame oil
1 tablespoon ginger, grated
1 bunch dill, chopped into ½-inch (1.3 cm) pieces
A few sprigs of fennel for garnish

Directions

- Bring water to a boil. Add the dry longan and cook on low heat for fifteen minutes.
- Heat a wok or skillet over medium-high heat. Add the oil. Just before it begins to smoke, add the ginger and stir-fry for one to two minutes, or until aromatic.
- Add the dill and continue stir-frying. Transfer the ginger and dill to the soup. Stir and cook for five minutes.
- Transfer to a warm soup bowl. Garnish with dill sprigs and serve hot.

Information

Dragon Eyes: A plum-sized tropical fruit called longan. When peeled, it looks like an eyeball, which is how it got the name "dragon-eye." It can be used in soups, desserts and candies, but it is best eaten fresh out of the shell. Chinese medicine considers the longan to be sweet and warm in nature. It tonifies the heart and spleen, nourishes the blood and calms the spirit. It also treats insomnia, palpitations, poor memory and dizziness. Sometimes it is placed under the bed of newlyweds in hopes of producing children.

Dill: An aromatic herb with a sweet and sour taste. The leaves and seeds are both edible. They aid the flow of energy, strengthen the stomach, chase away coldness and alleviate bloating caused by anger. They also act as a painkiller.

Dogs and cats actually blossom when switched to a meatless regimen, with glossier coats, fresher breath and cleaner teeth, more energy at play, and a more peaceful disposition.

—Jan Allegretti and Katy Sommers, *The Complete Holistic Dog Book*

4. Tofu Pouch Soup with Ginger

Makes 4 to 6 servings

Ingredients

10 ounces (300 g) dry tofu sheets
1 tablespoon black sesame oil
1 tablespoon ginger, grated
8 cups (2 quarts/liters) water
Salt to taste

Directions

- Rinse the dry tofu sheets and drain well. Cut each sheet into four small equal sections. Set aside.
- In a skillet, heat the oil and sauté the ginger for one to two minutes, or until aromatic.
- Add the water and bring to a boil. Add the pieces of tofu sheet and salt. Simmer for five minutes on low heat. Transfer to a warm soup bowl and serve hot.

Information

Black Sesame Oil: Made from black sesame seed. It is known for lowering the blood pressure and inducing uterine contractions. According to the *Record of Plants*, black sesame oil promotes physical strength, develops muscles, supplements brain marrow, strengthens tendons and bones, clears the hearing and vision, alleviates fear and constipation, lightens the body and slows down aging.

The Gods created certain kinds of beings to replenish our bodies; they are the trees and the plants and the seeds.
  —Plato, Greek philosopher (circa 428–347 B.C.)

5. Hot and Sour Chinese Soup

Makes 4 to 6 servings

Ingredients

5 dried shitake mushrooms

2 bags enoki mushrooms, trimmed and rinsed (see page 127)

4 cups bamboo shoots, peeled (if fresh) and sliced

1 Chinese cabbage, julienned

1 tablespoon oil

2 cups fried tofu skin, julienned

2 tablespoons low-salt soy sauce

2 tablespoons black vinegar

Pepper to taste

Toasted sesame oil

Thickener

2 tablespoons arrowroot powder

2 tablespoons cold water

Directions

- Soak the shitake mushrooms in hot water for twenty minutes, or until soft. Rinse well to remove the grit and squeeze out the water. Trim the stems and julienne.
- Bring water to boil in a pot. Add the bamboo shoots and return to a boil.
- Next add the cabbage. Reduce to low heat and cook for twenty minutes.
- Sauté the shitake mushrooms for one to two minutes. Add the enoki mushrooms, soy sauce, vinegar and salt. Cook for two more minutes. Transfer to the pot of soup and bring to a boil.
- Add the tofu. Reduce the heat to low and simmer for three more minutes.
- In a small bowl, mix the arrowroot powder with the cold water and slowly add to the soup. Simmer three more minutes until thickened, stirring frequently.
- Sprinkle with black pepper and drizzle with sesame oil.
- Transfer to a warm soup bowl and serve hot.

Information

Bamboo Shoots: A traditional forest vegetable in China for more than 2,500 years. Bamboo shoots are not only delicious, but are also rich in nutrients. They rank among the five most popular healthcare foods in the world. *The Compendium of Materia Medica*, a pharmaceutical text written during the Ming Dynasty (1368–1644), states: "Bamboo is slightly cold, sweet, non-toxic, and it quenches thirst, benefits the liquid circulatory system, supplements qi, and can be served as a daily dish."

> *I drank your milk when I was young.*
> *You ploughed my field when I was grown.*
> *Now that you are old and worn out,*
> *I will look after you.*
> —Ancient Chinese poem

6. Corn Chowder, Chinese Style

Makes 1 to 2 servings

Ingredients

4 cups (1 quart/liter) homemade
    broth or water
1 potato, peeled and diced
¼ carrot, diced
1 cup (8 oz/225 g) corn kernels
1 cup (8 oz/225 g) creamed corn
A few green peas
Salt to taste

Thickener

1 cup (150 g) flour
Oil (optional)
1 cup (8 fl oz/250 ml) homemade broth or water

Directions

- Pan-roast or sauté the flour in a heavy skillet over low heat, until slightly brown. Remove from heat and set aside.
- Bring three cups broth to a boil. Add the potato and carrot. Reduce the heat to low. Simmer for ten minutes, or until soft.
- Add the corn kernels, creamed corn, green peas and salt. Return to a boil.
- Mix the flour mixture with the broth and slowly add to the soup. Reduce the heat to low and stir continuously, until thickened.
- Transfer to a warm serving bowl and serve immediately.

Tip

Pan-roast a large quantity of flour that can be used later. Cool and store in an air tight container up to one month.

Information

Corn: Primarily known as a staple food and has many therapeutic properties. It is used in traditional Chinese medicine for treating urinary and kidney problems, lowering cholesterol and hypertension, preventing coronary heart and arteriosclerotic diseases, delaying cellular aging, and preserving cerebral functions. Corn silk can be made into a tea to cleanse the kidneys and the urinary tract. Parents will be happy to know that corn may be beneficial in the treatment of bedwetting in children.

Caution

Check the label on creamed corn. It may contain dairy products. Corn may be genetically modified, so it is best to use organic.

7. As-You-Wish Miso Soup

Makes 4 to 6 servings

Ingredients

1 bag enoki mushrooms, trimmed
    (see page 127)
4 cups (2 pints/1 liter) water
10 ounces (300 g) soybean sprouts
1 block silken tofu
    (12–16 oz/340–450 g), diced
1 teaspoon dry seaweed sprouts

Miso Sauce

2 tablespoons miso
1 tablespoon sugar or equivalent sweetener
2 tablespoons water

Directions

- Combine the miso and sweetener together with a little water. Set aside.
- Bring the water to boil and add the soybean sprouts. Reduce the heat to low and cook for ten minutes.
- Add the tofu and enoki mushrooms. Cook for five minutes.
- Add the seaweed sprouts and miso sauce. Cook for one minute.
- Transfer to a warm soup bowl and serve immediately.

Tip

If the miso is already sweet, do not add sweetener

Information

Seaweed Sprouts: An excellent source of protein, vitamins, minerals, carotene, chlorophyll and fiber. They balance and alkalize the body, remove metallic and radioactive elements from the body, and help to boost the immune system. They are rich in vitamin B2 and can prevent and cure a vitamin B2 deficiency, especially in the spring when diseases from a vitamin B2 deficiency become symptomatic. To prevent any loss of vitamin B2 in cooking, add a bit of vinegar. Seaweed sprouts can be found in Asian markets or ordered online.

As a man values his life,
So do animals love theirs.
Releasing life accords with the order of the universe;
Releasing life agrees with the teaching of the Buddha.
— Chu-hung, "Releasing Life," in Religious Vegetarianism

8. Classic Herbal Soup

Makes 4 servings

Ingredients

1 packet five-element Chinese herbs
3 homemade fried gluten balls
5 cups (1¼ quarts/liters) water
Salt to taste (optional)

Directions

Bring the water to boil in a medium-sized clay pot. Add the herbal packet and gluten balls. Reduce the heat to medium, cover and cook for fifty to sixty minutes. A rice cooker can be used instead.

Information

Five-Element Chinese Herbs: In Chinese culture, the five elements (fire, earth, metal, water and wood) are the fundamental elements of human health. This herbal mixture contains herbs that will nourish and balance the five elements in the body. The herbal packets can in found in Asian markets or ordered online.

To cultivate kindness is a valuable part of the business of life.
—Samuel Johnson, English author (1709–1784)

Kindness toward Animals

The Buddhist ideal is to live in harmony with animals and to respect the right of all living beings to live and be free. Every creature contributes something for the maintenance of the earth and our surroundings. Animals respond in a positive way to those who care for and protect them. In turn, those who show kindness to animals will naturally grow in compassion and live healthy and happy lives.

Buddhist monasteries have strict laws to protect wildlife and wildlife habitat. Setting fires to hills, woodlands and fields is prohibited, without reason, especially during nesting times. The isolated forest monasteries leave the wild animals and fish unharmed, so they naturally become nature reserves. In northwest America, Buddhists purchase virgin forests to prevent them from being logged and wildlife habitat destroyed. No hunting and fishing signs are posted. During hunting season, deer and birds take refuge in these territories. In times of drought, Buddhists have been known to rescue fish and turtles from ponds that are drying out, and transfer them to a river.

Old or sick livestock that would otherwise be put to death are sometimes released into the care of large monasteries that receive contributions for their upkeep. In America, someone learned that because of overpopulation, the government was running wild burros over cliffs. He bought two of the burros and offered them to the City of Ten Thousand Buddhas in California where they were cared for and pastured for the rest of their lives. Someone else purchased a cattle ranch in Montana and offered it to the monastery. The ranch, under the supervision of monks, has now become a rest home where the cattle graze there in peace.

The elimination of pests from crops for Buddhists, who refrain from using pesticides, presents a challenge. They often move the pests to a safe distance away and make sure they are provided with food. Extra crops are sometimes planted to share with pests. Another effective method used is to plant herbs and flowers among the vegetables to deter predators, such as planting white sage or lavender to keep deer away. Whatever method, Buddhists seek ways that will not cause harm to living beings.

Other ways that Buddhists engage in cherishing life is opening vegetarian restaurants and printing children's books on kindness to animals.

It is very significant that some of the most thoughtful and cultured men are partisans of a pure vegetable diet.

— Mahatma Gandhi, Hindu pacifist and spiritual leader, (1869–1948)

Around the third century B.C., when the Roman Empire began trading with the Chinese Han Empire, merchants brought the grindstone along the Silk Road to make pasta. For the first time, the Chinese began grinding wheat into flour and making noodles, dumplings, pancakes, stuffed buns, and steamed breads, calling them all *ping*.

Steaming hot, sweet-smelling,
Slurping them down—so tasty.
Soup, vegetables, noodles,
Delicious and easy for a busy day!
  —Dharma Realm Cookbook Team

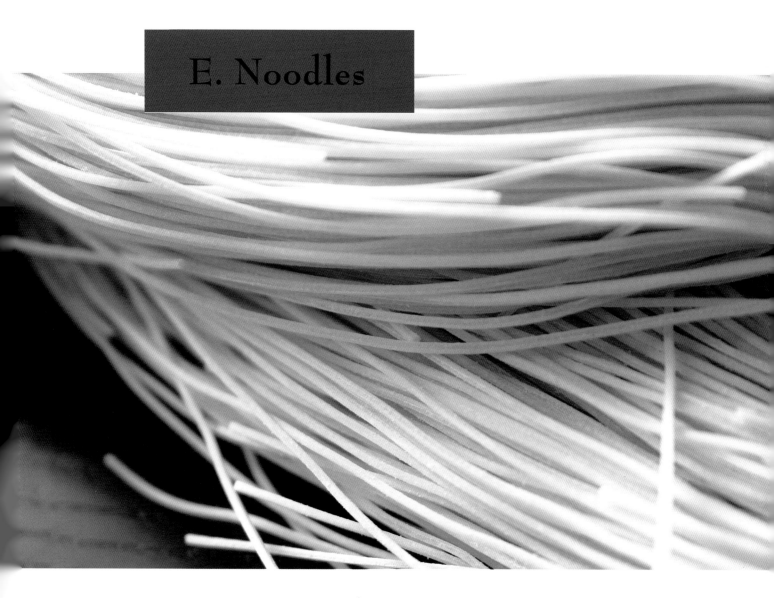

E. Noodles

1. Macaroni with Tomato Sauce, Chinese Style

Makes two servings

Ingredients

8 ounces macaroni pasta, cooked according to package directions

1 cup (1lb/ 250 g) string beans, cut into 1-inch (2.5 cm) pieces

Tomato Sauce

1 tablespoon oil

2 tomatoes, diced

½ tablespoon low-salt soy sauce

5 button mushrooms, sliced

Salt to taste

½ tablespoon sugar or equivalent sweetener

Tip

To make a delicious tomato soup, cook tomatoes and mushrooms in ample water. Season with salt and a sweetener, and add to cooked noodles.

Directions

- Blanch the string beans and set aside.
- Make the tomato sauce: Heat a wok or skillet over medium-high heat. Add the oil. Just before it begins to smoke, add the tomatoes and soy sauce. Stir-fry for three minutes, gently tossing. Add the mushrooms, salt and sweetener. Gently mix together. Reduce the heat to low. Cover and simmer for five minutes.
- Stir in the macaroni and mix well. Toss in the string beans and cook for one to two minutes or until well done, but still bright green.
- Transfer to a warm serving dish and serve immediately.

Information

Tomatoes: Chinese medicine classifies tomatoes as cooling in nature with a sweet and sour flavor. They relieve dryness, thirst, high blood pressure and headaches; cleanse the liver; purify the blood; and detoxify the body. The main nutrients in tomatoes are vitamin C and carotinoids that prevent arterial diseases and repress prostate cancer.

Caution

Green-picked tomatoes weaken the adrenals. They also upset the absorption of calcium. Those with arthritis should avoid them. Vine-ripened tomatoes are best.

Out of humanness and kindness, the ancient sages helped all creatures, caring for them and relieving their suffering. As humans, our hearts should be filled with humaneness.
—Dharma Master Di Xian

2. Good Luck Rice Noodles

Makes 4 to 6 servings

Ingredients

5 dried shitake mushrooms

1 package rice noodles

1 tablespoon oil

1 tablespoon soy sauce

½ cabbage, julienned

½ cup carrots, julienned

2 cups fried tofu pouches, julienned

6 cups (3 pints/1½ liters) homemade broth or water

10 ounces (300 g) mung bean sprouts

½ celery stalk, grated

½ teaspoon salt

1 teaspoon sugar or equivalent sweetener

¾ teaspoon pepper

Tip

If soy sauce is added at the end of cooking, the dish will have a sour taste. Add more soy sauce during the cooking time.

Directions

- Soak the mushrooms in hot water for twenty minutes, until soft. Rinse well to remove the grit and squeeze out the water. Remove the stems and julienne.
- Cook the noodles in boiling water for five to six minutes, or until they float on top. Drain and rinse in cold water.
- Heat a wok or skillet over medium-high heat. Add the oil. Just before it begins to smoke, add the mushrooms and stir-fry one to two minutes. Add the soy sauce and stir. Then add the cabbage, carrots and tofu.
- Continue to stir-fry until the cabbage is soft.
- Add the broth, salt, sweetener and pepper. Bring to a boil. Add the rice noodles and mung bean sprouts. Reduce heat to low. Using a pair of chopsticks or a fork, continue to stir-fry until the noodles are mixed well with the other ingredients and all the liquid has evaporated.
- Transfer to a warm serving dish. Top with celery and serve immediately.

Variation

Substitute chow mein noodles for rice noodles.

Information

Rice Noodles: When the five Mongol tribes invaded northern China, the Han people migrated to the south where they made rice strips that are now called rice noodles. In the early days, rice noodles were a delicacy, served only to guests of honor or during celebrations. During the Japanese occupation of Taiwan, eight kilograms of rice were exchanged for five kilograms of rice noodles. Rice was extremely valuable, but rice noodles were even more so.

3. Health and Longevity Noodles

Makes 4 to 6 servings

Ingredients

1 bunch Chinese thin noodles

1 quart/liter water

Jyun Kang Sauce

5 cups (1¼ quarts/liters) water

1 cup goji berries (see page 119)

1 cup dried longan (see page 138)

2 cups aged ginger, grated

1 slice dang gui

½ tablespoon cinnamon

2 tablespoon black sesame oil

1 tablespoon soy sauce

Directions

- Bring the water to boil in a medium-sized pot. Add the goji berries, longan, ginger, cinnamon, dang gui, sesame oil and soy sauce. Reduce the heat to low. Cover and simmer for forty minutes.
- Cook the noodles in boiling water until they are soft or float to the top.
- Drain and transfer to a warm serving dish. Pour the sauce on top of the noodles and serve immediately.

Tip

This dish is especially recommended for people who are cold-natured or for long-term vegetarians.

Information

Dang Gui: A medicinal herb that is grown in China, Japan and Korea. It is popular among women and often goes by the name "women's ginseng." It can also be taken by men. Its benefits include treatment for cardiovascular issues, constipation, insomnia, inflammation, and women's reproductive issues.

Are the blood and bones of sentient beings any different?
Who says that the life of one kind surpasses that of another?
You are advised to not shoot birds in trees;
The children in the nest are waiting for their mother.

—Bai Juyi (Tang Dynasty, 618–906),
    Sketches on the Protection of Life by Juan-Sou

4. Fragrant Noodle Soup

Makes 4 servings

Ingredients

20 lily flowers

10 ounces (300 g) bamboo shoots

4 cups (1 quart/liter) water

4 fried tofu pouches, julienned

3 pieces pressed tofu, flavored
with 5-spice powder

10 ounces (300 g) Shanghai bok choy,
chopped

4 bundles dried rice noodles

1 tablespoon low-salt soy sauce

½ tablespoon salt

½ tablespoon sugar or equivalent sweetener

Toasted sesame oil

Directions

- Soak the lily flowers for ten minutes and drain well. Remove the stems and julienne.
- Rinse the flavored tofu and julienne.
- If fresh, rinse and peel the bamboo shoots. Place in a pot of cold water and bring to a boil. Reduce the heat to low. Cover and simmer for ten minutes.
- Add the lily flowers, tofu pouches and flavored tofu. Bring to a boil. Add the soy sauce, salt and sweetener. Bring back to a boil. Remove from heat and set aside.
- Cook noodles according to directions on the package.
- Blanch the bok choy. Then add both the bok choy and noodles to the soup pot. Drizzle with sesame oil.
- Transfer to a warm serving dish and serve immediately.

Variation

For a thick soup, add the noodles and bok choy after cooking the bamboo shoots.

Tip

Cooking noodles separately enhances their flavor.

Green Leafy Vegetables: Contain vitamins and minerals that are essential for our bodies and also purify the blood. The Taiwanese Pharmaceutical Association recommends a daily consumption of one pound (500g) of green leafy vegetables.

I have no doubt that it is a part of the destiny of the human race, in its gradual improvement, to leave off eating animals.
— Henry David Thoreau, Walden (1817–1862)

5. *Hearty Tofu Pouch Sandwich*

Makes 1 to 2 servings

Ingredients

2 squares tofu pouch or plain tofu

1 tablespoon oil

3 slices whole wheat bread

4 slices tomato

3 lettuce leaves

2 tablespoons eggless mayonnaise

Directions

- In a skillet, heat the oil and sauté the tofu pouch squares until golden brown. Set aside.
- Spread the mayonnaise on one side of each slice of bread. Make a three-layered sandwich alternating between fried tofu pouch squares, tomato slices and lettuce. Cut into triangular halves.

Variations

Substitute avocado for fried tofu pouch or Japanese cucumber for lettuce.

Information

Raw Food: Eating small amounts of raw food can be helpful for cleansing and renewal. Lettuce alone helps with the absorption of nutrients and alleviates the burden on the stomach and intestines.

A Gift of Fourteen Cows

A young man named Kimeli, who had been studying in New York, returned to his village in Kenya. He was much troubled by the events of September 11, when three thousand people lost their lives in the collapse of the twin towers. He related the story of that tragedy to his people and told the elders that he wanted to offer his only cow to the American people. Kimeli's tribe, the Maasai, revere their cattle as a source of life. To them a cow is the most precious gift one can give. The elders agreed with Kimeli's wish. They invited a diplomat from the United States Embassy in Nairobi to visit the village where they greeted him with a full, sacred ceremony and presented him with not one but fourteen cows. Other villagers had joined Kimeli in his gesture of sympathy and solidarity with the American people. They took the suffering of the Americans into their own hearts.

These sacred, healing cows are still in Kenya, tended by a revered village elder who lives among them. They are distinguished from the other cattle by an earmark of two bars, representing the two towers. These cows will be kept under Maasai care and can never be slaughtered. The original fourteen have since calved and have now become thirty-five. They continue to be a symbol of hope and friendship from the Maasai to the American people.

For days and weeks after September 11, New Yorkers received sympathy messages from all over the world, but the gift of the cows touched their hearts in a way little else could. This story of compassion has been turned into a book for children, called *Fourteen Cows for America*.

CHINESE TRADITIONS
OF SUPPORTING HEALTH
AND PROTECTING LIFE

Healthy Eating throughout *the Seasons*

THE FIVE ELEMENTS IN COOKING

The theory of the five elements — metal, wood, water, fire, and earth — has existed since ancient times. The Chinese character for element means: to walk; to act; to travel. Used in this context, it means to follow the vital energy of the universe. The five elements are used to investigate the nature and function of all phenomena in the world. A human being's disposition will also determine one's fate and the environment one faces.

The following excerpts and information about the five elements are taken from three sources: *The Medical Classic of the Yellow Emperor*, lectures from the Venerable Hsuan Hua, March 1970, and *Healing with Whole Foods* by Paul Pitchford. *The Medical Classic of the Yellow Emperor*, translated by Zhu Ming, is an ancient medical text on health and disease that has been treated as the fundamental doctrinal source for Chinese medicine for ages; it is said to be written by the mythical Huangdi, the Yellow Emperor. *Healing with Whole Foods* is a book combining Asian traditions and the modern diet. Researched by an expert in the field, this book contains a wealth of information on health and diet as well as on ways to apply Chinese medicine and the five-element theory to a contemporary diet.

> *The workings of the heavens are sound while the superior man continually strives to be strong. People's daily routine should accord with the natural cycle of the universe, so the ideals of people and heaven would be as one. The lives of the wise accord with the four seasons so that cold and heat are avoided.*
>
> —The Medical Classic of the Yellow Emperor

Venerable Master Hsuan Hua says, "The five flavors, sour, sweet, bitter, pungent and salty, correspond to the five elements. Sour corresponds to wood, bitter to fire, pungent to metal, salty to water and sweet to earth. If you understand the nature of medicinal herbs, you will see that the heart, liver, spleen, lungs, and kidneys are also classified according to the five elements. The heart is associated with the predominance of fire, the liver is associated with the predominance of wood, the spleen and stomach are associated with the predominance of earth, the liver is associated with the predominance of metal and the kidneys are associated with the predominance of water. In the human body, the heart, liver, spleen, lungs and kidneys are connected with metal, wood, water, fire, and earth.

In the spring, don't eat much of the sour flavor. You will get liver sickness and the eyes cannot see clearly. In the summer, don't eat much bitter. It will harm the heart. In the late summer, you can eat more of the sweet flavor with no harm. A little sweet is good any season, but don't overdo it. In the autumn, do not eat much of the hot flavor. You will get lung sickness. In the winter, do not eat much salt. You will get kidney sickness. Eating too much in any season is not good. Don't overdo it, and you won't get sick."

In *Healing with Whole Foods*, the author points out that nourishing our lives according to the times of year is an important principle in health, ensuring a healthy body and fewer illnesses. Each season affects the body differently, requiring different nutrients. In the spring, one should eat lightly, in the summer, one should eat foods that are sweet and cooling, in the autumn, one should eat cleansing foods, and in the winter, one should eat foods that are substantial and warming. A balance of *yin* (cooling) and *yang* (warming) should be the goal for a healthy and happy life, so that debilitating energies are kept at bay.

SPRING — THE WOOD ELEMENT

Sour foods correspond to wood and spring.

> *Spring is the time to rise early in the morning, take brisk walks; loosen your hair, and enliven your spirit…the supernatural forces of spring create wind in the heavens and wood upon the Earth. Within the body, they create the liver and the tendons… the color of green…they give the voice the ability to make a shouting sound, and create the eyes, the sour flavor, and the emotion anger.*
>
> — The Medical Classic of the Yellow Emperor

Venerable Master Hsuan Hua says, "In the springtime you shouldn't eat too much sour food. Why? Wood flourishes in the spring. If you add more of the sour nature, it becomes even more flourishing. 'Isn't it good to be more flourishing?' you might ask. Too much is the same as too little. Going too far is the same as not going far enough; then we need to make up the deficiencies in our body. Wood is in command in the spring, because it is when all the myriad things come forth. Sour-flavored foods are associated with the liver. You can eat a little, but not too much. Sour food will injure your liver. When the liver is injured, you won't be able to see things clearly, since the liver influences the eyes."

According to *Healing with Whole Foods*, in the spring the appetite for food decreases and the body naturally cleanses itself. The diet should be the lightest of the year, and foods should reflect the rising and active nature of spring—fresh, young greens and sprouts. Salty and heavy foods eaten in the winter should be limited at this time, or they will clog the liver, resulting in fevers and spring fits.

The vegetables that grow in the spring naturally contain the sour taste and have properties that eliminate the winter heat, thin the blood, and clarify the vision, resulting in a smooth flow of energy in both the body and mind. These are asparagus, rape, spinach, celery, shepherd's purse, goji berries, romaine lettuce, parsley, pea pods, watercress, radish, and turnip greens. The temperature is still relatively low during early spring. Children, elders and those who are weak should keep warm to avoid contracting viruses. Simmer orange peels, kumquats, turnips, pears, or water chestnuts to make a tea and drink it frequently.

To harmonize the flow of liver energy, *The Medical Classic* recommends the sweet and pungent flavors of young beets, carrots and other sweet starchy vegetables; wheat and barley, mung beans, tofu, green peas, prunes, tangerines, peanuts, black sesame seeds, and also grains — legumes and seeds — that are sprouted and then cooked or eaten raw. Raw foods and sprouts renew the liver and encourage great vitality and strength. However, if raw foods are eaten in excess, they can weaken the digestive system and bring about excessive cleansing. Sweeteners such as barley malt, date sugar, molasses and rice syrup also stimulate the energy flow. The pungent flavor can also be found in cooking herbs—basil, fennel, marjoram, rosemary, caraway, dill, and bay leaf.

Disharmony in the liver is caused by too many desires—for sex, money, fame, food, and sleep. Since these desires are never fulfilled, one feels empty and is driven to overeat. The energy in the liver cannot flow and becomes stagnant. Vinegar mixed with honey is the most common and powerful remedy to reduce stagnancy in the liver. The recipe is one part vinegar to one part honey per cup of water. Lemon, lime, or grapefruit can be substituted, but they act more slowly.

Spring is the time to stabilize the emotions and give attention to self-awareness and self-expression. One should be at ease in body and mind, yet dynamic like the energy of spring; devoid of anger and frustration and have no thoughts of killing, stealing, and harming others. In this way, the emotional and physical energy of the liver will be harmonized and will flow smoothly.

Spring Cooking: Cook for a shorter time in spring but at a high temperature. Vegetables should not be thoroughly cooked, especially the inner part. When sautéing or stir-frying, do so quickly over high heat. When cooking with water, steam lightly or simmer minimally.

SUMMER — THE FIRE ELEMENT

Bitter foods correspond to fire and summer.

> *The supernatural forces of summer create heat in the Heaven and fire on Earth.*
> *Within the body, they create the heart [and small intestines] and the pulse . . .*
> *the red color, the tongue, and the ability to express laughter...they create the*
> *bitter flavor and the emotion of happiness and joy. . . .*
>
> —The Medical Classic of the Yellow Emperor

Venerable Master Hsuan Hua says, "Summer corresponds to the flourishing of fire. It's very hot in the summertime, so fire flourishes. Someone may say, 'You say summer is hot, but when you go to Australia, the summer month of June is the coldest time of the year.' That's because seasons differ in countries to the north and south of the equator. In the summer, we should not eat too many bitter things. We can eat a little bitter but not a great deal. Why is bitterness said to be associated with fire? No matter what kind of food it is, if you burn it with fire and then eat it, it tastes bitter. Bitterness is associated with the heart."

Healing with Whole Foods states that summer is a time of growth—a time to be joyous, to work, play, travel and volunteer your services to help others. Excessive sweating causes the body to lose water and minerals, resulting in weakness, if they are not replaced. To prevent heat stroke, one should drink hot liquids and take warm showers. This will induce sweating and cool the body. Drinking too many liquids, however, dilutes the digestive system and weakens the heart. Eating cold food (ice cream) and drinking iced drinks should be avoided. They contract the stomach and stop digestion. One's stomach should be 98.6 degrees for good digestion.

The author recommends eating more cooling and watery foods in the summer, like melon and salad greens. The water in vegetables and fruit is naturally pure and nutritious. It has a "life-giving" property that cannot be found even in drinking water. Winter melons are the most cooling, followed by yellow cucumber, gourd, luffa, finger citron melon, bitter melon, watermelon and others. Tomato, eggplant, celery, lettuce, asparagus, watercress, dill and basil also belong to the 'cool' type of vegetables. Summer fruit include: sweet and juicy plums, peaches, papayas, mangoes, and pineapples. Eating a variety of light soups and drinking leaf and flower teas made from chrysanthemum, mint, chamomile, and rose hips with vitamin C, calm the nerves and neutralize toxins.

The bitter aspects of wheat, brown rice, oats and barley calm and focus the mind and prevent excessive thoughts and worry. These bitter aspects of grain are found in their germ and bran, which are unfortunately removed during the refining process to make white rice and white flour. To receive the benefits of grains, eat them in their whole state.

In both Western and Eastern healing, it is thought that the heart not only regulates blood circulation, but also serves as a mental and emotional center. It controls the consciousness, spirit, sleep, memory, and according to Chinese healing, it houses the mind. The Chinese character for heart (*xin*) is translated as heart-mind. Many doctors say that most heart diseases begin in the mind.

Summer Cooking: Make brightly colored salads and dishes with a variety of summer fruit and vegetables. Decorate with flowers and cut the vegetables into decorative shapes. Cook lightly and spice-up the dishes a little with pungent and fiery flavors. Steam or simmer over high heat for a short time, or sauté or stir-fry quickly. Use a little salt, more water and less oil in cooking. Heavy, greasy, salty food causes sluggishness. On the hottest days, cook and eat outside or have a picnic.

LATE SUMMER —
THE EARTH ELEMENT

Sweet foods correspond to earth and late summer

> *The supernatural forces of late summer create moisture in the Heaven and fertile soil upon the Earth; they create the flesh within the body and the stomach [and spleen and pancreas]. They create the yellow color...and give the voice the ability to sing...they create the mouth, the sweet flavor and the emotions of anxiety and worry.*
>
> —The Medical Classic of the Yellow Emperor

Venerable Master Hsuan Hua says, "The element Earth is associated with the center, but spreads out to all four seasons. The earth has the ability to nurture; it nourishes the Way. Late summer is a time to settle down and live simply and harmoniously between the two extremes, the middle way. Earth's related organs are the stomach and the spleen-pancreas, which are primarily responsible for the digestion and distribution of food and nutrients. The energy and essences extracted from digestion are used by the body to create qi energy (immunity), vitality, warmth, and formations of the tissues and mental functions."

In *Healing with Whole Foods*, the author says that late summer is the last month of summer and the middle of the Chinese year. It is considered to be the interchange of all seasons, the point of transition from yang (heat of summer) to yin (cool of fall). During this time, the sunshine is fierce and the rain falls in drizzles. The focus is on hot and humid or dry, depending on where you are. He recommends that in order to attune to this time of the year, one should choose foods that are harmonizing and represent the center — mildly sweet foods, yellow or golden foods, round foods and foods like millet, corn, carrots, cabbage, garbanzo beans, soybeans, squash, potatoes, string beans, yams, tofu, sweet potatoes, sweet rice, rice, amaranth, peas, chestnuts, filberts, apricots, and cantaloupes. Food must be chewed well for ultimate digestion.

In many cultures, the transitional seasons are times for purification. A short, three-day single-grain fast, or a vegetable or fruit fast brings about an easy-flowing transition from late summer into fall.

Late Summer Cooking: Use moderation with a mild taste as a guide to late summer cooking. Avoid making complicated dishes with unusual combinations. The dishes should be simple with little or no seasonings. Minimize cooking time and use a moderate amount of salt, oil, and water.

FALL — THE METAL ELEMENT

Pungent foods correspond to metal and autumn.

> *The forces of autumn create dryness in Heaven and metal on Earth; they create the lung organ and the skin upon the body… and the nose, the white color, and the pungent flavor, the emotion grief, and the ability to make a weeping sound.*
> —The Medical Classic of the Yellow Emperor

Venerable Master Hsuan Hua says, "Autumn is associated with metal. At this time we should not eat too many pungent (hot, spicy) things. If we eat too many pungent things in autumn, we will injure our lungs. In the fall, all things in nature begin to contract and move their essence inward and downward. Grains ripen, leaves fall, seeds dry and hillsides begin to lose their green color. It is the harvest season, a time to gather and store food and plan for the approaching coldness of winter. Fall is a transition stage: 'yang (warmth) disappearing and yin (coldness) lengthening.' After the 'white dew,' the rain slackens off and the weather becomes drier. It is hot during the day and cold at night. Winds and cold air can invade the body, making it easy to catch a cold or the flu, thus, 'fall of many problems.' Protect yourself well, and do not wear too much or too little."

Healing with Whole Foods suggests offsetting the dryness of fall by decreasing the intake of hot, spicy foods, which disperse the energy and cause coldness in the body. One should eat more foods that moisten the body such as soybean products, barley, millet, pear, apple, persimmon, loquat, seaweeds, black and white fungus, potatoes, sweet potatoes, almond, pine nut, peanut, sesame seed, barley malt, rice syrup and a little salt in cooking to moisten dryness. Consideration should be given to eating fewer yin or cold foods such as salads. Watermelons, muskmelons, and papayas should be avoided in the fall, because they deplete the yang energy in the body and harm the spleen and stomach.

Eating sour foods in moderation in the fall gathers the scattered energies from summer and focuses the energy inward for winter--freshly baked sourdough bread, sauerkraut, olives, pickles, aduki beans, sesame seeds, walnuts, pecans, white fungus, spinach, eggplants, vinegar, Chinese hawthorne, tofu, sour apples, grapes, pomegranates, star fruit, lemons, grapefruits, persimmons, pears, longans, and rose hips tea. Eating too much sour food can be harmful.

The colon is paired with the lungs and its function is to eliminate what is no longer needed. Grief and sadness are the emotions associated with the lungs and colon. Their energy is also characterized by holding onto principles and keeping commitments, but letting go when necessary without emotional repression. In Chinese healing, the condition of the lungs and colon is determined by how well we 'hold on' or 'let go.'

A mild lung or colon cleansing once a year can eliminate toxic build-up from the summer heat and from the environment; it can also clear grief and sadness. Foods with the pungent flavor that assist in both cleansing and protecting the lungs and colon are: turnips, ginger, horseradish, cabbage, and white peppercorns. Mucilaginous foods are also important for protection, such as seaweeds, marshmallow root, flaxseed and fenugreek. Foods that bolster immunity and protect against lung and colon cancer are dark green and golden-orange vegetables, rich in beta-carotine: carrots, winter squash, pumpkins, broccoli, cauliflower, kale, mustard greens, watercress, and wheat and barley grass.

Fall Cooking: Cook with less water, at a lower heat, and for a longer time. Use a little salt in cooking to moisten dryness. Heighten the diet with pungent flavors and hearty foods that are sautéd, stir-fried, or baked. Foods like winter squash and roots thicken the blood for cool weather. Eat fewer cold foods such as salads and fruit during the fall. Stew or bake apples and pears. Make cold-pressed salads by blanching greens and pressing out the water.

WINTER —
THE WATER ELEMENT

Salty and Bitter foods correspond to water and winter.

> *The forces of winter create cold in Heaven and water on Earth; they create the kidney organ and the bones within the body... the black color, and the salty flavor, the emotion fear, and the ability to make a groaning sound.*
>   —The Medical Classic of the Yellow Emperor

Venerable Hsuan Hua says, "Winter is associated with water. We should not eat too many salty things in the wintertime. If we eat too much salt, it will harm the kidneys. If you know the principles of regulating and balancing the five flavors, you will find that this is the best method for staying healthy. It is more effective than taking any amount of vitamins. No matter what kind of food it is, you shouldn't eat too much. If you eat too much, not only will it not be beneficial, it will actually be harmful. The stomach of a human is approximately the size of a quart. Overeating causes the stomach to enlarge.

"Water is all-pervasive. It can support the earth and encompass the heavens, nourishing all things. The brightness of the sun and moon is supported by water. Water does not contend; it simply flows downward to the lowest places."

Healing with Whole Foods points out that winter marks the end of all four seasons. The yin energy is the strongest while the yang energy is the weakest. When the energies reach their extreme, the human body faces the invasion of chills and winds, which enter the kidneys most easily and can cause numerous illnesses. This is the time to keep the kidneys warm, suppress the yin and protect the yang so that the ability to resist colds is raised.

Foods with the salty and bitter flavors are appropriate for winter. They cool the exterior of the body and bring the body heat deeper and lower. Whole grains such as rye, oats, quinoa, sorghum, amaranth, and even sweet brown rice contain the bitter flavor. Vegetables include: lettuce, watercress, endive, escarole, turnips, celery, asparagus, alfalfa, carrot tops, parsley, ginger, kale, brussels sprouts, cabbage, and the outermost leaves of cabbage. Fruit includes: dried longans, lychee, red dates, citrus, and citrus peels. Nuts include: walnuts, chestnuts, pecans, and sesame seeds. Roasted ground chicory (used in coffee substitutes) also contains the bitter flavor.

The salty flavor is found in miso, soy sauce, seaweeds, salt, millet, and barley. Use salty foods with care, because salt tightens the kidneys and bladder, causing coldness. Drinking too much water also weakens these organs and affects the heart as well.

The black color corresponds to the water element. Foods such as black rice, black beans, black sesame, black dates, black fungus, and all kinds of seaweed create harmony in the kidneys. Yellow vegetables such as carrots, lilies, peanuts, yams, and winter squash nurture the kidneys and strengthen the blood veins. Spices for warmth include: cloves, fenugreek, fennel seeds, anise seeds, star anise, black peppercorns, ginger, and cinnamon bark.

In the winter, since we wear more clothing, stay in heated rooms and exercise less, we easily accumulate heat in the body, and the lungs may become congested. To keep the body and lungs clear, we should eat some cooling foods such as radish, Chinese cabbage, celery, spinach, bamboo, oranges, tangerines, persimmons, pears, and apples.

Winter Cooking: Cook foods longer, at lower temperatures and with less water. Make warm hearty soups and steam winter greens to fortify the kidneys. Roasted nuts and baked apples are good on cold days.

Note on ginger: Ginger contains the pungent flavor; stimulates blood circulation; warms and relaxes the kidneys in cold weather and clears the lungs in fall. It should be avoided or used sparingly in spring and summer.

THREE TRADITIONAL MEASURES FOR GOOD HEALTH IN WINTER

- **Eat congee.** Nutritionists of ancient times advocated eating hot congee (rice porridge) on cold winter mornings. Adding red dates and red beans to the congee will also keep us warm and multiply our energy. The Chinese have a tradition of eating red bean congee on winter solstice, January 8, and eating a congee made of eight items on lunar January 25.

  Oatmeal congee nurtures the heart and eliminates frustration. Carrot congee aids digestion and acts as an expectorant. Yam congee supplements the lungs and stomach. Walnut congee nurtures the yin and stabilizes the essence. Large date congee increases energy and nourishes yin. Corn congee increases the appetite. Sweet potato congee nourishes the liver and kidneys.

- **Eat plenty of warming foods** to balance access to yang and yin. Eat dried longans, dates, yams, red beans and glutinous (sweet) rice. Overweight individuals should avoid fatty, sweet, rich foods.

- **Eat nuts, seeds, and black foods** such as: walnuts, Chinese chestnuts, pine nuts, pecans, peanuts, sunflower seeds, sesame seeds, seaweeds, black beans, and black rice. A Chinese maxim says: "Take supplements for twenty-seven days after the winter solstice and enjoy freedom from sickness and pain the coming year." These foods, in appropriate amounts, increase our immune system's ability to resist diseases. In cold weather, our skin becomes thinner and we perspire less, making it easier to store nutrients—all of which lay an excellent foundation for good health.

Since the greenhouse effect is becoming more and more serious, the four seasons in Taiwan are becoming less distinct, but the way to health through diet remains the same, adjusting the diet to accord with each person's conditions and the weather. Rely on local, seasonal foods that accord with nature; imported foods are expensive, often processed, and contain preservatives. Avoid eating refined food. The more refined food we eat, the further away we are from health and attaining our goals in cultivation.

It is our hope that you will use this cookbook as a guide to the world of Chinese vegetarian cooking and gain insight into the wisdom imparted. Regarding your food sources, may you not only nourish your own happiness, but contribute to peace in the world.

AN INTRODUCTION TO THE DHARMA REALM BUDDHIST ASSOCIATION

Founder: Venerable Master Hsuan Hua.

Taking the Dharma Realm as its substance, DRBA seeks to disseminate the true principles of Buddhism to all areas of the world. Its mission is to translate the Buddhist sacred texts, to teach the orthodox Dharma, to promote ethics-based education, and to bring benefit to all sentient beings.

The guiding principles of DRBA are: no contention, no greed, no seeking, no selfishness, no looking for personal advantage and no lying.

In addition to the City of Ten Thousand Buddhas, DRBA has nearly thirty branch monasteries located throughout the United States, Canada and Asia. DRBA's Sangha members honor the rules and practices established by the Buddha: eating one meal a day, always wearing the precept sash, observing the precepts and being mindful of the Buddha, studying the teachings, practicing meditation, living together in harmony and dedicating their lives to Buddhism.

DRBA's institutions include the International Institute for Translation of Buddhist Texts, the Institute for World Religions, Sangha and Laity Training Programs, Dharma Realm Buddhist University, Developing Virtue Secondary School and Instilling Goodness Elementary School, and others.

The doors of DRBA's monasteries and institutions are open to anyone from any country who wishes to devote him or herself to the pursuit of humaneness, justice and ethics, and to the discovery of their true mind.

Works Cited

Allegretti, Jan and Sommers, Katy. *The Complete Holistic Dog Book: Home Health Care for Our Canine Companions.* Berkeley: Ten Speed Press. 20013. Print.

Campbell, Colin. *The China Study.* Dallas: BenBella Books. 2006. Print.

American Heart Association. *Sea Salt vs. Table Salt*
www.heart.org/HEARTORG/GettingHealthy, May 12, 2014

Briggs, Mark. *Top 10 Alternatives to Sugar.* www.theecologist.org.

Langre, Jacques de. *Seasalt's Hidden Powers.* Magalia, California: Happiness Press. 1987. Print.

Li, Shih-Chen, Smith, Porter F., and Stuart, George Arthur, editors. *Chinese Medicinal Herbs.* Mineola, New York: Dover Publications. 1973. Print.

Maoshing, Ni. *The Yellow Emperor Classic of Medicine.* Boston: Shambala Publications. 1995. Print.

McDougall, Dr. John. *The McDougall Program.* New York: Plume Books.1991. Print.

PCC Natural Markets. *Choosing the right cooking oil.* www.pccnaturalmarkets.com.

Phelps, Norm. *The Great Compassion: Buddhism and Animal Rights.* New York: Lantern Books. 2004. Print.

Pitchford, Paul. *Healing with Whole Foods.* Berkeley: North Atlantic Books. 2004. Print.

Robbins, John. *Diet for a New America.* Belvedere Tiburon, CA: HJ Kramer, New World Library. 1987. Print.

Robbins, John. *The Food Revolution.* Berkeley: Conari Press. 2001. Print.

Shaw, Hank. *Hunt, Gather, Cook: Finding the Forgotten Feast.* New York: Rodale. 2011. Print.

Silverstone, Alicia. *The Kind Diet.* Emmaus, Pennsylvania: Rodale. 2011. Print.

Shywan, Lin Ching. *A Buddhist Perspective on Vegetarianism, Vegetarian Cooking—Chinese Style.* online.sfsu.edu. 1995. Web.

Stamets, Paul. *Mycelium Running: How Mushrooms Can Help Save the World.* Berkeley: Ten Speed Press. 2005. Print.

Sure, Heng, translator. *Kindness: A Vegetarian Poetry Anthology*. Burlingame, California: Buddhist Text Translation Society. 2004. Print.

Sure, Heng. *Whole Body Vegan Lifestyle*. Burlingame, California: Buddhist Text Translation Society. 2005. Print.

The Organic Consumers Association. *SAFETY GUIDE*, May 2009. www.organicconsumers.org

Veith, Ilza, translator. *The Yellow Emperor's Classic of Internal Medicine*. Berkeley: University of California Press. 2002. Print.

Wagstaff, Jesse D. *International Poisonous Plants Checklist: An Evidence-Based Reference*. British Royal Horticultural Society, CRC Press. 2008. Print.

Walters, Kerry S. and Lisa Portmess. *Religious Vegetarianism*. New York: State University of New York Press. 2001. Print.

Wu, Nelson Liansheng and Wu, Andrew Qi Wu, translators. *Plain Questions: Yellow Emperor's Canon of Internal Medicine*. Beijing: China Science and Technology Press. 1979. Print.

Zibdeh, Nour. MS, RD. *The Low Down on Agave, Honey, and Date Sugar*. www.nourition.com, August 5, 2010.

Reliable Websites:

www.acupuncture.com

www.archure.net/salus/vegquotes

www.cancer.org Diet and Nutrition

www.changeforayear.com/socrates-buddha-einstein

www.chineseherbshealing.com/ginkgo-nut

www.greenlivingnewsletter.com

www.health.harvard.edu,

www.japanesefood.about.com

www.livestrong.com/enoki-mushrooms

www.naturalmedicinalherbs.net

www.notable-quotes.com

www. nutritionfacts.org

www.sierrapotomac.org

www.thechinastudy.com

www.thefreedictionary.com/shitake

www.veganforum.com

www.veganhealth.org

www.veganoutreach.org

Dharma Realm Buddhist Association Branches

World Headquarters
The City of Ten Thousand Buddhas
2001 Talmage Road
Ukiah, CA 95482 USA
tel: (707) 462-0939
fax: (707) 462-0949
www.drba.org
(Branch URLs and email addresses
are available on the DRBA website.)

U.S.A.
California
Berkeley
Berkeley Buddhist Monastery
2304 McKinley Avenue
Berkeley, CA 94703 USA
tel: (510) 848-3440
fax: (510) 548-4551

Burlingame
The International
Translation Institute
1777 Murchison Drive
Burlingame, CA 94010-4504 USA
tel: (650) 692-5912
fax: (650) 692-5056

Long Beach
Blessings, Prosperity,
and Longevity Monastery
4140 Long Beach Boulevard
Long Beach, CA 90807 USA
tel/fax: (562) 595-4966

Long Beach Sagely Monastery
3361 East Ocean Boulevard
Long Beach, CA 90803 USA
tel: (562) 438-8902

Los Angeles
Gold Wheel Monastery
235 North Avenue 58
Los Angeles, CA 90042 USA
tel: (323) 258-6668
fax: (323) 258-3619

Sacramento
The City of the Dharma Realm
1029 West Capitol Avenue
West Sacramento, CA 95691 USA
tel: (916) 374-8268
fax: (916) 374-8234

San Jose
Gold Sage Monastery
11455 Clayton Road
San Jose, CA 95127 USA
tel: (408) 923-7243
fax: (408) 923-1064

San Francisco
Gold Mountain Monastery
800 Sacramento Street
San Francisco, CA 94108 USA
tel: (415) 421-6117
fax: (415) 788-6001

Maryland
Avatamsaka Vihara
9601 Seven Locks Road
Bethesda, MD 20817-9997 USA
tel/fax: (301) 469-8300

Washington
Index
Snow Mountain Monastery
PO Box 272
50924 Index-Galena Road
Index, WA 98256 USA
tel: (360)799-0699
fax: (815)346-9141

Seattle
Gold Summit Monastery
233 1st Avenue
West Seattle, WA 98119 USA
tel: (206) 284-6690

Canada
Alberta
Avatamsaka Monastery
1009 4th Avenue
S.W. Calgary, AB T2P OK, Canada
tel: (403) 234-0644

British Columbia
Gold Buddha Monastery
248 East 11th Avenue
Vancouver, B.C. V5T 2C3, Canada
tel: (604) 709-0248
fax: (604) 684-3754

Australia
Gold Coast Dharma Realm
106 Bonogin Road
Bonogin, Queensland AU 4213
Australia
tel: 61-755-228-788
fax: 61-755-227-822

Hong Kong
Buddhist Lecture Hall
31 Wong Nei Chong Road,
Top Floor
Happy Valley, Hong Kong, China
tel: (852) 2572-7644
fax: (852) 2572-2850

Cixing Chan Monastery
Lantou Island, Man Cheung Po
Hong Kong, China
tel: (852) 2985-5159

Malaysia
Dharma Realm Guanyin Sagely
Monastery
161, Jalan Ampang
50450 Kuala Lumpur, Malaysia
tel: (03) 2164-8055
fax: (03) 2163-7118

Prajna Guanyin Sagely Monastery
Batu 51, Jalan Sungai Besi
Salak Selatan
57100 Kuala Lumpur, Malaysia
tel: (03) 7982-6560
fax: (03) 7980-1272

Fa Yuan Monastery
1 Jalan Utama
Taman Serdang Raya
43300 Seri Kembangan
Selangor Darul Ehsan, West Malaysia
tel: (03)8948-5688

Malaysia DRBA Penang Branch
32-32C, Jalan Tan Sri Teh Ewe Lim
11600 Jelutong
Penang, Malaysia
tel: (04) 281-7728
fax: (04) 281-7798

Guan Yin Sagely Monastery
166A Jalan Temiang
70200 Seremban Negeri Sembilan
West Malaysia
tel/fax: (06)761-1988

Taiwan
Dharma Realm Buddhist Books
Distribution Society
11th Floor
85 Zhongxiao E. Road, Sec. 6
Taipei 115, Taiwan R.O.C.
tel: (02) 2786-3022
fax: (02) 2786-2674

Dharma Realm Sagely Monastery
No. 20, Dongxi Shanzhuang
Liugui Dist.
Gaoxiong 844, Taiwan, R.O.C.
tel: (07) 689-3717
fax: (07) 689-3870

Amitabha Monastery
No. 136, Fuji Street, Chinan Village,
Shoufeng
Hualian County 974, Taiwan, R.O.C.
tel: (03) 865-1956
fax: (03) 865-3426

Subsidiary Organizations
Buddhist Text Translation Society
City of Ten Thousand Buddhas
4951 Bodhi Way
Ukiah. CA 95482 USA
web: www.buddhisttexts.org
email: info@buddhisttexts.org
catalog: www.bttsonline.org

Dharma Realm Buddhist University
City of Ten Thousand Buddhas
4951 Bodhi Way
Ukiah, CA 95482 USA
www.drbu.org

Dharma Realm Outreach
City of Ten Thousand Buddhas
outreach@drba.org

Instilling Goodness and
Developing Virtue School
City of Ten Thousand Buddhas
2001 Talmage Road
Ukiah, CA 95482 USA
www.igdvs.org

Institute for World Religions
2245 McKinley Avenue, Suite B
Berkeley, CA 94703 USA
web: www.drbu.org/iwr
email: iwr@drbu.org

Religion East & West (journal)
2245 McKinley Avenue, Suite B
Berkeley, CA 94703 USA
tel: 510-848-9788
web: www.drbu.org/iwr/rew

Vajra Bodhi Sea (magazine)
Gold Mountain Monastery
800 Sacramento Street
San Francisco, CA 94108 USA